GRAINING THE MARE

THE POETRY

OF

RANCH WOMEN

•

EDITED AND WITH PHOTOGRAPHS
BY TERESA JORDAN

GIBBS·SMITH

PUBLISHER

SALT LAKE CITY

First edition
98 97 96 95 94 10 9 8 7 6 5 4 3 2 1
Introduction copyright © 1994 by Teresa Jordan
Poems are copyrighted by the individual poets. Permissions to reprint are cited on page 152.
Photographs copyright © 1994 by Teresa Jordan

This is a Peregrine Smith Book, published by
Gibbs Smith, Publisher
P.O. Box 667
Layton, Utah 84041

Design by Kathy Timmerman, White Space Design Inferno, Minneapolis

Cover art: *Blue Ball Horses* by Donna Howell-Sickles, © 1990

Printed and bound in the U.S.A.

Library of Congress Cataloging-in-Publication Data

Graining the mare: the poetry of ranch women / [compiled by] Teresa Jordan.
       p.   cm.
    ISBN 0-87905-640-1
    ISBN 0-87905-626-6 (pbk.)
    1. Ranch life—West (U.S.)—Poetry. 2. Women ranchers—West (U.S.)—Poetry.
  3. American poetry—Women authors I. Jordan, Teresa.
    PS595.R37G73   1994
    811.008'03278—dc20   93-34686
                            CIP

For Hal, my one true love

CONTENTS

INTRODUCTION

THIS BOOK GATHERS TOGETHER THE POETRY OF thirty-five women from ranch culture, ranging in age from their early twenties to their nineties. Nearly two-thirds of the women make all or most of their income from raising some combination of cattle, sheep, and crops on ranches in the Western United States and Canada, or they did so for a substantial part of their adult lives. Some of these were born to the work; others came to it on their own or married into it. Of the remaining third, most were raised on ranches but left at adulthood or after a first marriage—some departed with great reluctance; others fled. A couple of the women featured here were raised in town but grew up close to the land because of grandparents or other relatives. A few have been involved more exclusively with horses than with cattle or sheep.

Their poetry has a raw intensity that comes when voices emerge where there has been only silence before. Born out of intimate relationships to land and animals, to weather and seasons, to friends and family, these poems are true to the heart, close to the earth, and unflinching. This is fresh poetry, nourished by both beauty and crisis. Rural women have only recently begun to write this honestly about their lives.

THE TRUTH IS, RURAL WOMEN HAVE ONLY RECENTLY begun to write publicly about their lives at all, at least in any number. When I was compiling the bibliography for *Cowgirls*, an oral history of women on ranches and in rodeo that was published in 1982, I could find fewer than three dozen first-person narratives by women in ranch culture, published over a period of

eighty years. Only three of those— Elinore Pruitt Stewart's *Letters of A Woman Homesteader* (1914), Agnes Morley Cleaveland's *No Life for a Lady* (1941), and Nannie Alderson's *A Bride Goes West* (1942), were well known. I located only one ranch novel written by a woman that had realistic women characters—Peggy Simson Curry's *So Far From Spring*, which was based in part on the lives of women she had known growing up on a ranch in North Park, Colorado. There were books that I didn't learn about until later—Mary Clearman Blew's collection of short stories, *Lambing Out* (1977); Marguerite Noble's novel, *Filaree* (1979); and Gwen Petersen's humorous *Ranch Woman's Manual* (1976) to name a few—but women's voices were rare and hard to find.

I wasn't looking for poetry at that point, but had I been, I would have found the pickings leaner yet. Several horse and cattle magazines carried occasional poems by women, and I might have been lucky and stumbled upon Martha Downer Ellis's *Bell Ranch Glimpses* (1980), a compilation of four earlier books of her poetry. I knew of Peggy Simson Curry's *Red Wind of Wyoming and Other Poems* (1955), which had been republished so many times it had become something of a legend in my home state of Wyoming. But there was no tradition of women's poetry parallel to that of cowboy poetry; there were no ballads women recited to each other over coffee or on the long rides to distant pastures; certainly most of the ranch women I knew would not have considered the dailiness of their own lives as material worthy of verse.

If I had been particularly acute, I might have picked up rumblings that this was about to change. If I had lived in South Dakota, I might have heard about the poetry of ranch woman Linda Hasselstrom which was just beginning to appear in literary magazines. If I had still lived in Wyoming, I might have run across a slim volume of poems by Gretel Ehrlich, a documentary filmmaker who had moved to the state and started working as a ranch hand, or I might have heard about the appointment in 1981 of Peggy Simson Curry as Wyoming's first Poet Laureate. And if I had followed Mrs. Curry's story and had fully understood it, I might have known that women's voices were just beginning to burst forth in new and powerful ways, and that when they did they would be met with surprising acceptance by both women and men.

The day of Mrs. Curry's appointment, a reception was held at the governor's mansion with the members of the Wyoming legislature and their spouses. Mrs. Curry was asked to read some of her work. "She had planned to read some of her favorite landscape and nature poems," wrote Mary Alice Gunderson in the introduction to *LandMark*, a collection of Mrs. Curry's short stories, "but overcome with the emotion of the day and the honor she had received, she lost her voice." Her friend, poet Charles Levendosky, agreed to read for her and she indicated to him her selections. Then, at the last minute, she nudged him and whispered for him to include another, "Jack Patton":

Jack Patton, Commander of rakers in the hay field,
Jack Patton, General of my thirteenth summer,
Jack Patton cursing me on hot afternoons . . .

"If you do it, do it right," he says. . . .

[I] Wished him all manner of evil:
Lord, give him loose bowels squatting in a ditch
before the President of the United States.
Lord, make him have pimples on his face the size of
 horse turds.
Lord, let his penis fall off, be eaten by a million flies.

All my life remembering, "If you do it, do it right."

Later, Mrs. Curry would say that she didn't know what got into her. This was not, after all, language that nice ladies used before the Wyoming legislature. But the assembly burst into enthusiastic applause and afterwards "Jack Patton" was the poem people wanted to take home.

Since that time, a whole new literature has sprung forth from women on the land. Some who were just beginning to write ten years ago have gained national recognition. Since 1984, Linda Hasselstrom has published three volumes of poetry and three of essays, including *Windbreak* (1987) and the award-winning *Land Circle* (1992); Mary Clearman Blew has published a second collection of stories, *Runaway* (1990), and a memoir of her Montana ranch family, *All But the Waltz* (1991), both to great acclaim; Gretel Ehrlich's *Solace of Open Spaces* (1985) has become a classic and she has since published several more books. But nowhere has the proliferation of women's voices been more pronounced than in poetry.

When the first Cowboy Poetry Gathering was held in Elko, Nevada, in 1985, only six out of twenty-eight featured poets were women. Several of them recited cowboy classics and, with few exceptions, their original work tended either to be patterned after the traditional male poems, both in style and content, or to be humorous and sometimes self-deprecating looks at women's particular folly in a mostly male domain. None of this was surprising. The tradition of recitation, of poems drawn from men's stories and performed by men, went back over a hundred years in the American West and its roots, grounded in Anglo-Saxon and other balladeering cultures, were much older. There was no such tradition for women. In addition, ranch women shared with other women the muteness about their real knowledge and concerns that Tillie Olson wrote about in *Silences*: "the silence of centuries as to how life was [and] is."

Cowboy poetry has enjoyed a renaissance, and today, a decade after that first event, there are over 150 gatherings a year in a dozen western states. While recitation of classics is still important, there are a phenomenal number of ranch people writing new poetry, and much of it, particularly the poetry by women, is breaking new ground. At the Elko gathering—still the largest one, with an attendance each year of over 8,000—the all-women sessions are among the most popular and women are well integrated into the rest of the program as well. Some, such as Gwen Petersen, whose work was featured at the first Gathering, write traditional rhymed and metered verse; others, such as Marie Smith, another early participant, and Sue Wallis, write both rhymed and free verse; and some, such as Thelma Poirier and Linda Hussa, write free verse only. All are drawing on their own experiences and ways of seeing to develop a poetry that is decidedly female, alive with energy, freshness, and courage. The cowboy poetry movement did not give birth to this body of work, but it has nourished it, providing a climate for deep friendship, inspiration, and experimentation. Approximately half the women in this book are frequent or occasional participants in cowboy poetry gatherings all over the West.

•

WHEN I LOOK BACK ON MY CHILDHOOD AND YOUNG adulthood on a ranch in southeastern Wyoming, I realize that I knew early that women inhabited secret territories. I often had the sense of living in two worlds—a sense which is shared by many ranch women I know. There were few girls in the neighborhood my age, so I mostly played with my older brother and his friends. I was a consummate tomboy: I played cowboys and Indians, I wrestled, I swore. As much as I annoyed the boys, I made sure they could never say I was a quitter or a fraidy cat. I hated dolls and dresses, and one Christmas I cried all day because my great-grandmother—who knew that the only thing I really wanted was a bazooka—had given me a handcrafted doll carriage.

But when I had girls for company, the play was altogether different. I never grew to like dolls, but I loved the camaraderie of girls in the great outdoors, where we inhabited a separate and quite magical world. When I was with boys, we rode horses. When I had girls to play with, we actually became horses.

With girls, it didn't matter if we played in the front yard, galloping and neighing as we chased each other in circles, or if we saddled up real horses and headed out from the house. Our horses were not just vehicles, they were intimate friends. We sometimes forgot entirely that we were human, or that a saddle separated us from the huge beasts who carried us, and I can still remember that magical moment of transcendence when we first nudged our horses into comfortable lopes. Suddenly my own chubby awkwardness would fall away and I would be sleek and strong and graceful. It would be my neck straining forward, my hooves that were striking the ground. I would know I could run forever.

Inside the house I had a similar sense of living by two sets of rules. Our home was often full of people as the community gathered after a branding or weaning or other shared labor, and I remember standing in the dining room, listening to the deep rumble of the men's voices in the living room and the softer murmur of the women in the kitchen, trying to decide which world to step into.

No men ventured into the kitchen, but some women found a place in the living room. These were the women who worked outside, who could handle a rope, who knew about the treatment for diphtheria or poison weed. I was proud to be one of them, to have earned the right to sit in, and I liked the men's hard, clear stories of adventure in the outside world, of horses they had ridden or bullies they had stared down. Sometimes the women who sat in the living room told stories, too, but we were careful to say nothing that might endanger our place among the chosen; we kept our secrets. We might talk about riding horses, but we didn't talk about our separate ways of seeing them. And when we joined the women in the kitchen, we entered into another secret territory, the interior landscape of family, community and self.

Part of the energy of this new poetry from ranch women comes, I suspect, from the fact that much of it is charting those mysterious lands. Although the work is still evolving, much of it clusters around three topics, none of which were considered the stuff of literature only a decade ago: women's particular and sometimes transcendent identification with nature; their relationships with family and communi-

ty; and women's roles, both contemporary and histori-
cal, in ranch culture.

In Judy Blunt's "Sisters," two girls watch from the
corral fence as the men rope an unbroke colt for the
older sister. When the horse is thrown and tied, the
older girl is

beside herself in love
with the shine of sun tan flanks, snowy
stockings tied in a bunch, the baby fringe
of mane and tail to match. When she reached up
and drew me off the fence, her hands shook
like the colt's own hide and I forgot
the unfair edge of luck and age she held
eight years over my head. We hunkered
down close enough to touch, our faces
and the clouds behind us mirrored
in the dark, wild eye of her colt.
Cream Puff, she said, glancing back
for fear the men would hear and laugh,
I'm going to name her Cream Puff.

The connection that many women feel to animals
is transcendent, yet seldom sentimental. In Linda
Hussa's "Under the Hunter Moon," the narrator
stalks a coyote that has ravaged her flock:

Slain lambs, guts ripped open
Magpies and blow flies
Blatting ewes with swollen bags searching the flock

A lamb a day for two weeks
    I grip the rifle tighter

The narrator comes upon the coyote in play:

I watch her snatch mice out of the grass
    flip them up like popcorn,
    down the hatch. She is a comic
    this coyote, playing, laughing
    making her way steadily toward me
    my finger soft on the cold steel trigger

The narrator and the coyote lock eyes on each
other, and in the final three lines of the poem, which I
won't reveal here, lie the whole complexity of the nat-
ural world, where one life often weighs against another.

Linda Hasselstrom's "Beef Eater" draws on a
related complexity, that of eating the animals you
love. The narrator's preparation of a beef heart is
unflinching and yet filled with tenderness, echoing
the husbandman's cycle of nurture and slaughter:

I split the maroon shape
lengthwise,
open it like a diagram, chambers exposed.
I cut tough white membranes off valves . . .

Gently,
I lift the full heart
between my hands,
place it in the pan
with its own blood, fat juices.
I roast that heart
at three hundred fifty degrees
for an hour or two.
Often I dip pan juices,
pour them lovingly over the meat.

When the heart is ready, the poet smiles as she
takes it to the table:

My friends have begun to notice my placid air,
which they mistake for serenity.
Yesterday a man remarked on my large brown eyes,
my long eyelashes,
my easy walk.

I switched my tail at him
as if he were a fly,
paced
deliberately
away.

Edith Rylander acknowledges in a different way
the transcendence of a life that takes full responsibil-
ity for the cost of its survival: "We can sleep through
the whole night now," she writes at the end of "Out to
Grass," the last of a series of poems that capture the
exhausting work of lambing season. "We can study to
make our lives / Worthy of what they eat."

Often women draw parallels between the lives of the animals they love and their own. In "Graining the Mare," Jo-Ann Mapson sympathizes with a horse who has just slipped a colt:

It was less than a thrill
watching the stud do his work:
chains, hobbles, both horses panic-eyed,
handlers turning sheepish, her tail
stiffly arced in defiance.

March sky: empty, gray,
barren as this horse.
Whatever do we expect, falling
for mustaches like shades of lipstick?
"Honest, he's different this time for sure,"
the chorus we sing in any weather.

•

THE MORE INTERIOR WORLDS OF FAMILY, COMMUNITY and self make up a second hidden territory explored in these poems, one that may be even more difficult to map—often it hides the secrets we were raised never to reveal. Marriage has long been the source of humor in rural culture, as when Jeane Rhodes describes her husband's reaction to the chokecherry jelly she labored for hours to make:

This morning my husband beamed over his plate
Of sausage and pancakes, and said as he ate,

"The best thing about this syrup to me
Is that these nice berries are utterly free."

To show that I'm tolerant and kind and forgiving—
The man that I live with is still with the living.

But these women are not afraid to write about the depth of love, and also of loss. "Love, my love, you are not gone from me / for I see you in the face of all the land," writes Marie Smith in her lovely poem of grief, "Finding." Elizabeth Ebert describes a moment of recognition in "Song from the Day the Pump Broke":

I watched him through the dusty plumber's glass:
The mud-caked jeans, unshaven face,

The squinting eye. He looked so very tired
—and *old!* My heart caught in my throat
And through the quick hot tears I saw
My life's one verity, the pivot point
On which my world revolves:
I love you, and I always will, my dear.

Many poems deal with the inner workings of family and the rituals of generational teaching, as when Sue Wallis describes how her mother (Myrt Wallis, whose poetry is also featured in this book) taught her about calving:

Thus my Mama's mother taught her, and then my mama
   taught to me
The important things of birthing and of Life and Nature's
   ways—
Of the knowledge wise and female—first so given to me
   free
By my mother in a pasture on those long-passed calving
   days.

The passing of information from one generation to another is not always easy, and Thelma Poirier captures the pain of father and son in "sorting cattle":

your son shouts, move out
move out of the way . . .
you should have known you could not build a corral
large enough for both of you

These poems mention, too, the things that until now were rarely spoken of in rural communities— alcoholism, abuse, the marriages that don't work. In Doris Bircham's "leaving," a woman hangs out the wash and thinks about a neighbor who left her husband. "Could it have been . . . that night / he came home drunk / the burden of his anger / clenched inside his fists?" she asks.

I continue this simple task
of hanging clothes   thinking
how little I know
about where they go
between one wash and the next

how there's no place to hide
the worn places, the three-cornered rips
how no bleach has been made
that can remove all the stains

Sometimes these women write about the difficulties of their own lives—the broken loves, unrealized dreams, and loneliness. Some of these poems are painful; others are salty. Here's a fragment of Sue Wallis's "Coyote Bitch":

Tonight . . .

I feel like a Coyote Bitch
(in heat)
Do not annoy me, tempt me, or toy with me
I have been lonely too long.

•

THE FINAL TERRITORY MAPPED IN THESE POEMS MAY have been the most secret of all until recently, and that is how we view ourselves and how we are viewed as women—a landscape that has shifted tremendously over the past few years. Peggy Godfrey captures the frustration of many ranch women who see their skills discounted when she writes of Old Vogal:

He assured me I was lucky
That my bales were done up tight
Lucky that I caught the dew
And chanced to bale it right.

This poem of four short verses is light and humorous, easy to digest, but it is also the work of a quiet revolutionary. It has been reprinted in several publications and is magnetted to refrigerator doors all over the West.

Hand in hand with a more open claiming of their own place, ranch women have claimed their female ancestors. As the biographer Carolyn Heilbrun has suggested, the "ultimate anonymity" is to be storyless. Anglo women in the West were just that until recent decades: as late as 1976 a major textbook on the history of the West was published that listed the names of only three women in its index. There has been a tradition of reverence to female pioneers,

sometimes taking the form of sentimental paeans to the "backbones of the West," carved into statues of sunbonneted Madonnas or read at historical celebrations. But only recently, with the publishing of virtually hundreds of pioneer women's diaries, letters, and memoirs—and the searching out of other records that many of the women in this book have undertaken on their own—have individual lives come into clear enough focus to provide the stories we seemed to have hungered for. If one thing surprised me as I read over submissions for this anthology, it was the number of poems inspired by the stories of earlier women. These are not poems of faceless reverence but of deep empathy and fascination with particulars. In "Flowering Almond," Jane Candia Coleman recalls a visit with a neighbor:

. . . I read your diaries,
sixty years of valley history recalled . . .

> The white leghorns laid today.   First time.
> The eggs were fine.
> Went up the creek, cut wood, drove the wagon down.
> Bought 18 dozen clothespins at the store.
> The baby died. Ground so hard we dug all day.
> The paint mare foaled a brown stud colt.
> My almond tree put out a flower.
> Two dry years and cattle dropping.
> I lug water to the tree and pray . . .

What lies in my lap is the coming and going
of lives and seasons; a ritual,
as the twilight whirling of wild babies,
as the branch of your almond tree
laid lightly down along the split rail fence
each spring for years.

Native American women have kept better hold on the stories of their past, and Navajo poet Luci Tapahonso passes on this image of her grandmother:

Yes, it was my grandmother
who trained wild horses for pleasure and pay.
People knew of her, saying:
> She knows how to handle them.
> Horses obey that woman.

She worked,
skirts flying, hair tied securely in the wind and dust.
She rode those animals hard and was thrown
time and time again.

•

"HOW DO WE TELL THE TRUTH IN A SMALL TOWN?"
asked North Dakota author Kathleen Norris in a
recent front-page piece in the *New York Times Book
Review*.[1] "Is it possible to write it? . . . A writer who
is thoroughly immersed in the rural milieu . . . faces
a particularly difficult form of self-censorship. . . .
[She] must either break away or settle for producing
only what is acceptable at a mother-daughter church
banquet or a Girl Scout program."

Anyone who has lived in the country or in a
small town knows what Norris is talking about, and I
suspect that the poets featured here have all struggled
with it to greater or lesser degree. As Linda Hogan
writes in "Other Voices":

There are things we do not tell
when we tell about weather
and being fine.
Our other voices take sanctuary
while police with their shepherds
stand guard
at the borders of breath
lest our stories escape
this holy building
of ourselves.

Yet ranch women have broken through, if only
the past few years, and some of the poems in this
book are startling in their honesty. "If I Left," writes
Penelope Reedy,

. . . the gals at the supermarket
over coffee and a smoke
would say they knew it
would come to this
". . . her, with 'the big head and all.'" . . .

And if I stay
until he shoots me,
catches me in the act of poetry,
barricaded behind a wall of books,
the Women's Auxiliary would say,
"She drove him to it."

As Norris suggested, some women have to break
away to tell the truth, and Penelope Reedy had to
leave rural culture in order to claim her own life.
Other women did not, though they might have been
able to write about personal difficulty only after their
situation had changed. Peggy Godfrey describes
humorously the "Perfect Wife" her second husband
and she could use to get their life in order, and then
notes:

I've chopped away her personhood
To get this "perfect wife."
It makes me sick to realize
This joke was once my life.

One purpose of storytelling in Navajo culture is
to restore our spirits to the state of "hohzo"—beauty
or harmony. Luci Tapahonso's poem "In 1864" tells
the story of the 8,354 Navajos who were forced to
walk from Navajo Country to Bosque Redondo (Fort
Sumner) and were held prisoner there for four years.
Over 2,500 of them died. When the narrator finishes
the story, her daughter is weeping:

. . . Then I tell her that
It was at Bosque Redondo the people learned to use
    flour and now
fry bread is considered to be the "traditional" Navajo
    bread.
It was there that we acquired a deep appreciation for
    strong coffee.
The women began to make long, tiered calico skirts
and fine velvet shirts for the men. They decorated their
    dark velvet
blouses with silver dimes, nickels, and quarters.
They had no use for money then.
It is always something to see—silver flashing in the sun
against dark velvet and black, black hair.

1 "A Crowded Writer on the Lonely Prairie," by Kathleen Norris, *New York Times Book Review*, December 27, 1992, pps 1+.

The poem tells us we must never forget or deny the past. "You are here / because of what happened to your great-grandmother long ago." But in even the most painful past, there is beauty. The poem restores a sense of harmony through the very act of honesty.

Much of the work in this collection strives toward that end. It looks at the realities of rural life in all its joy and its pain—truly, honestly, without elaboration or denial. And through that keen look, we have the ability to live more fully. "I'm quite prepared to leave old cruelties behind," wrote Thelma Poirier in a recent letter, "but not 'old beauty.'" These poems are acts of beauty. They prove that we can tell the truth and survive.

Sally Bates

Ride to the Cattle
by Sally Bates

The ashes lie smirking
The hearth holds its tongue
Thoughts swing from right then to wrong
Words lightly spoken
Now promises broken
He's gone, he rides to the cattle

Given to grieving
Is lighter than leaving
No matter the hours alone
With tenderness near
His heart wasn't here
He's gone, he rides to the cattle

To tie him to traces
Of my favorite places
A cruelty bitter as gall
It's hard in the spring
But death in the fall
If my cowboy can't ride to the cattle

Lying lonely and still
Hear the wild whippoorwill
The sun cracks the sky with the dawn
Horses to nurture
A life to endure
He's gone, he rides to the cattle

His shadow will crawl
On my blankets come fall
Leaves blowin' through dirty windows
Will his heart ever learn
Will he ever discern
That my love lets him ride to the cattle.

SOME MIGHT THINK BEING BORN and living in one place all your life would be boring, limiting, and certainly not a way to live life to the fullest. Perhaps, for some, that would be true. Not for me. My roots are five generations deep and they have made me a part of Arizona, part of Yavapai County, and a part of what happens here. Some folks aren't real partial to words. They prefer action and pictures and being in the midst of what's happening. I have always loved words, and the amazing fact that they convey our deepest feelings and beliefs, if we find a perfect way to write or say them. I haven't found those perfect ways yet, but I have found joy in the writing.

Virginia Bennett

MY HUSBAND AND I ARE JUST about to move to a new job in Washington. We've been in Oregon over a year, and it hasn't worked out. We tried two jobs, and neither place kept their promises about housing. After spending the last four months in a twenty-four-foot travel trailer, we've decided to move on.

What has been an eye-opener for me through all this is to realize that we have actually chosen our lifestyle. I guess we've been doing that all along, but we weren't aware of it. As we sat in that little old trailer, we considered our options. Pete thought a lot about renting a place somewhere and getting a job driving truck or welding or working as a mechanic—all skills that he is good at and could get high wages for. I hated the thought of leaving ranching, but it seemed like we had to do something. Just in time, we found the job in Washington. We won't make the good money, but at least we'll be doing what we love and have been doing for the last twenty years. We made a choice to stay on the ranch, and that thought sustains me through a lot.

For Grampa
by Virginia Bennett

So, now it's come down to this:
You live on in a picture on the wall.
Tho' you died maybe 30 years ago,
it doesn't seem that long at all.
Not so long ago that my dad and I
went to visit you in your camp.
I can still smell your pipe, the apple-wood smoke,
and the coal oil from the lamp.

We called it a camp, but it was where
you lived out your life on borrowed ground.
You had a wind-up clock, I'm sure of that,
I can still remember the sound.
And in my black and white photograph,
fuzzy, as in a dream,
frozen in time, you are mowing hay
with a well-fed, pure white team.

"Grampa," I begged, "make the horses jump!"
and I was sure that you would.
So you whistled them in from the juniper field,
they bounded up through the wood,
where at the pole gate in the dry stone wall
you'd left the lower rail standing.
In their race for the barn, they flew the rail
and lightly touched in landing.

I marveled at what a trainer you must be
that your horses would come to your tune.
And we stood in the barn full of cob-webs while
they crunched grain in that Yankee afternoon.
I don't recall a hug, a kiss or touch,
yet, I didn't think you were cold.
That's just the way my Grampa was:
quiet, wise and old.

Another picture, and you're with your
Ayshire oxen, back in '34.
Again, you are mowing, no one played
back then, just livin' was a chore.
So much that I recall are just
stories told me long ago
of a common man, not a hero, but
I wonder, where did you go . . .

Before I had the chance to know you,
to be brave enough to talk?
Just think of the tales that we could share,
Of paths that we would walk.
But I was just a gangly kid
that day you had to go away.
If I could hear your voice once more,
would you approve of me today?

For you must know that blood between us
is not easily understood.
For I make stone walls, I work with horses
and I do it halfway good.
But I didn't know you long enough
for you to really impress.
I was just a little, rugged girl
with a Grampa for a hero, I guess.

The Tough Goodbye
by Virginia Bennett

He stood there by the windmill, and gazed out over his spread.
Then, remembering the facts, he shook his grizzled head.
Even tho' he felt true ownership in every sense of the word,
He'd never really owned this ground, and those cows were not his herd.

The events of the last few weeks seemed to gently insist
That in all his wildest dreams, he never thought it'd come down to this.
For thirty years, he'd run this outfit; he'd brought it back from the skids.
His good dog was buried here, and it was here he'd raised his kids.

But he'd only been on the payroll, and he'd thought that was enough
'Til the owner died, the son took over, and the market got too rough.
So, a realtor came to the ranch one day and pounded in a sign,
And the foreman looked the other way, prayin' that God would be kind.

It took a couple years to sell, as the old man hoped it might,
Until the prices of cattle and land coincided just right.
A big corporation from Texas bought it; added it to their pool . . .
Imported their own manager . . . an ag student right out of school.

I guess the old man was prepared for it—I guess he saw it comin'.
He'd bought five acres and a trailer house, with electricity and plumbin'.
He told everyone it was his ace in the hole—his port in case of a storm,
But when he went there, it didn't feel like home, in any shape or form.

So, now, today was movin' day, and his stock trailer was loaded down.
And he'd sold his last good gelding to a team-roper up in town.
Already the new, young manager was eagerly movin' in.
Anxious for the old man to leave so his managin' could begin.

Under his breath, the foreman cursed the fool, and walked out to the tower,
And wondered why it should work this way, who had the right or power?
His blood and sweat were in this ground; he was the one who should stay.
Why, he was the one who, for thirty years, was here each night and day.

He'd weathered the blizzards, fed the hay, was here for better or worse,
He'd doctored colts, helped first-calf heifers, encouraged calves to nurse.
Yes, in many small and subtle ways, he and this ranch were married,
Especially after his wife had left—it'd been ten years since she was buried.

And now fate has dealt this strong man one final bitter hand.
For courts do not count sweat and blood as titles to any land.
In your eyes, for him to leave, why, there shouldn't be anything to it,
But as he heads for his truck he knows, it'll take all he's got to do it.

Doris Bircham

I WAS RAISED ON A MIXED FARM (we raised both crops and stock) and I attended a one-room country school. After training to be a nurse, I returned to the Cypress Hills area of southwestern Saskatchewan, married a rancher and have been a working partner in our cattle operation for over thirty years. We have a son and a daughter, both married and both ranching in the area. My writing began as an on-again, off-again hobby, but in the past few years I've taken more time for it. The role of ranch women is so unique and challenging, and to me so rewarding, that I find myself wanting to share some of my ranch-life experiences with others.

Coffee Row
by Doris Bircham

They gather each morning
at the back of the old store
where a window
outlines grass-fringed slopes
and patchwork strips.

Joe Blostenik has never missed
Tuesday's cattle auction or a rodeo
since he stepped out of his stirrups
eight years ago.

And Hank whose asthma
drove him early
to his house in town
wheezes each slow step
to the end of the street.

They listen to the tap
of old Bill's cane
the tap as repetitious
as his tales of the thirties
that ride cigarette smoke
across the room.

These men who meet
stir past dreams inside their cups
and are never more than a window
or one last story
away from the land.

weaning time

by Doris Bircham

she rides with the men as morning sun
cuts a path along the horizon's edge
her horse lopes easy over frosted grass

at the bottom of a coulee
she gathers cows and calves
points them towards the open gate
Hurry up her son yells
as one cow cuts past her
make that horse get a move on
and his words bite deeper
than the October wind

through swirling dust
at the back of the corral she helps
sort heifers from steers, pushes calves
one by one up the rough plank chute

she scrapes manure from her boots
hurries to the house, checks the roast
peels potatoes and remembers
calving time and the stormy spring night
she yanked the tough membrane
from a new calf, then compressed its chest
until it gave its first gasp, she recalls
other storms and the January blizzard
the night her son was born

at the auction ring
she takes a seat by her husband
rubs sweaty palms on her jeans
as their steers fill the ring, she watches
the line of her son's jaw tighten
then start to relax as the bids come in

back at home that night she walks out on the step
hears cows calling for calves that don't answer
yet when she glances across the yard she's drawn
to shadows and panels of moonlight
beginning to fill the empty corral

After the Funeral
by Doris Bircham

my aunt and I are drinking coffee
with him in his kitchen
it has been five days
since the jaws of life opened
his daughter's new car

he's been working more hours
than usual in his shop
I can see the line
where his welder's cap
creases his brow   sadness
hides in the shadows under his eyes

I can cry, he says, not just at night
but any hour of the morning
or afternoon   sometimes
there's no way I can stop

it's not until we're driving home
that my aunt says,
men have come a long way
it's okay now for them to cry
and I say, maybe we're the ones
who've travelled enough distance
to let them

leaving

by Doris Bircham

you were hanging diapers
two long rows of whites
on your backyard clothesline
that day which was the first of many days
we folded laundry together

now I hang a plaid shirt by the hem
my arms heavy with the weight
of your leaving

my mind replays conversations
looks for answers hidden

was it that call from the bank
the fourth in one week

could it have been the day
you were kept after work
and your youngest daughter
tried to make supper and met you
at the door with her tears
and her scalded hand

or was it that night
he came home drunk
the burden of his anger
clenched inside his fists

sadness folds around me
while I search
for you   for ways to reach out
and find the ragged edges
of your pain

I continue this simple task
of hanging clothes   thinking
how little I know
about where they go
between one wash and the next
how there's no place to hide
the worn places, the three-cornered rips
how no bleach has been made
that can remove all the stains

Afton Bloxham

M Y RANCH LIFE BEGAN WHEN my husband realized that a desk job wasn't his bale of hay. When an opportunity arose as manager for Hod Sanders' first ranch at Big Sandy, Wyoming, we packed up kids and dogs and headed for the hills. That was the beginning of thirty-five years—nine ranches in five states—all for the same employer. That's probably a record of some kind. For a town girl, it was quite an abrupt change. But whenever there was something that had to be done, I pitched in. I learned—the hard way—on most everything: driving cows, feeding a hay crew of twenty-five, cleaning up after hired families moved out, aide to the bovine and equine vet problems. You name it—I did it.

What Counts Most
by Afton Bloxham

I often wish that I could be
like my friend Carolyn, for she
is strong and she can do
most anything that she needs to—
like heft a bale, or fix the plow,
or break a colt, or rope a cow.

What a weak stick poor Heck got,
for strong and daring I am not!
Oh, there are many things I've done,
like run the swather sun to sun,
and brand, and vaccinate, and things
that being wife to Hector brings.

But staring down a raunchy beast,
or riding broncs till I'm deceased,
or fixing sections on the knife
is not the suit for this ranch wife.
Nor stretching wire till it's taut,
nor stacking bales. But it is not
the things I cannot do that count,
for I tell Heck that no amount
of hammer pounding strength could be
worth just the joy of having me.

Judy Blunt

Sisters
by Judy Blunt
for Margaret

One whine shy of a forced march
to the pickup, I hung a long face
between the third and fourth rails
of Jack's Larb Hills cow camp corral,
picking at scabs of dry Lodgepole bark,
watching Crooked Cross riders sort
bands of broomtail mares and yearling colts
bred to buck. A fidget alongside the men,
my older sister waited, grown-up in stiff
boots, straw hat brim clean and barely
crimped, her knuckles braided white
around a pint-sized hackamore.

The round corral stormed with colts cut
from the main herd, Jack pivoting slow
and sure, center of a pinwheel blur
of bays and roans, reds and wall-eyed
blacks, his lariat coiled in one leather glove.
He pulled a loop and snaked it low past
future Cannonballs and Widow Makers, snagged
both front feet of a palomino filly,
popped the slack and dropped her flat, breathless.

When the others took the open gate
the filly lay still in the dirt, dazed
and hog-tied—too light to buck, Jack said,
and quartered like a cow horse. My sister
didn't hear a word, beside herself in love
with the shine of sun tan flanks, snowy
stockings tied in a bunch, the baby fringe
of mane and tail to match. When she reached up
and drew me off the fence, her hands shook
like the colt's own hide and I forgot
the unfair edge of luck and age she held
eight years over my head. We hunkered
down close enough to touch, our faces
and the clouds behind us mirrored
in the dark, wild eye of her colt.
Cream Puff, she said, glancing back
for fear the men would hear and laugh,
I'm going to name her Cream Puff.

AFTER THIRTY-TWO YEARS ON A ranch, first as a kid and then as a wife, I'm now a single mom, a writer, a full-time graduate student, and I work twenty-five hours a week sanding hardwood floors. Writers who are childless, who have a separate room and scheduled time to write, who have a spouse's income to help them through the lean times, may well look upon my life in horror. For all things massive and minor, the buck stops right here—at a desk an arm's reach from the front door, two leaps from the telephone and the length of one sprawled child from the television set. I wear earplugs, the kind the cops use on the firing range. I write between bells and buzzers. I write while the house rocks on its springs like a loaded cattle truck. But if I write in spite of my children, even more I write because of them. Being a single parent has given me a drive, a reason why okay is not good enough, and my reward comes when this intensity and focus shine through a poem or an essay.

Josephine Hall

by Judy Blunt

She got a good turn-out as funerals go,
it being July and the first cuttin' down
and no rain since June. Those years
a man made as much in church as on a plow
but even so, they were restless,
thumb-warping new creases in their hats
and straining a furtive rain watch
through the purple stained glass prism
of Mary crying at the feet of Jesus.
Salt of the earth women settled the pews
like crows in a cornfield, picking
at the crimp of Sears & Roebuck corsets
through their best righteous black,
dabbing their eyes with hankies
tatted at the Ladies Club crochet and tea
socials. They all looked quickly
on the coffin, and away, knowing
Josie took strange a year ago, quit
going to meetings, and turned plain words
odd, when she spoke at all. Even so
when the Reverend called it the will of God,
no one looked sideways. They buried her
and talked of other things at the Midale Hall
hot dish potluck following. The men eased
collar buttons, squatted on their heels
tracing fuel-line and crankshaft patterns
on the silty floor. Wives ran dustrags
over the tables and set out food, chasing
the ghost of Josie Hall with words born
drowning in their own echo, loud life
goes on words, covering the fear. What if
tomorrow some other one of us
hears voices in the dirty wind.
What cloud will we be weighing
when she walks into rows of withered corn
dragging the butt of a 30.06
and only her babies,
ground-tied to the edge of the field,
crying come back,
come back.

At the Stockman Bar, Where the Men Fall in Love, and the Women Just Fall
by Judy Blunt

Black Velvet shots and water back,
I tell the creep who tries one sleazy
hand on my ass, but I'll buy my own—
tougher than hammered owl shit fella,
that's me, and he says he hears a Real
Woman calling for him somewhere
down the bar. The shot glass wobbles
in my fingers until I'm safe
at my own back table, transparent
in the crowd. By now they're paired off
and packed to static frenzy, stomping
boots and upraised arms fanning high
clouds of smoke against the ceiling,
foam and ice cubes slung around, so
damn much fun. The lead man's singing
Crackers in Her Cleavage, a love song
I think, and one girl Gets Down Bad,
her own long hair in her mouth,
dancing like a dog shakes a rat.

The man she's with already has his
shirt off, and he whips it over
their heads so hard the pearl snaps
crack and pop like fingers will, but
louder. I look away when Creep
walks by and prods my ashtray. Blow
ten bucks on perfume then waste it
with a ten-cent cigarette, he says,
says he could teach me a few things.
I waltz with someone like my dad,
then grab my coat and find my way
outside, the pull of booze and music
dragging stars down too low and hot
to wish on, lifting the street up
to meet my heels. I smell it first,
Limburger cheese, then see the car
festooned with toilet paper and stupid
shaving cream words that don't make sense.
Balloons bob and weave from the back
bumper, caught like a bride's bouquet.

I could take them all, but I pick
a blue one, break its string, and let it
rise over the street lights, balanced
on the breeze and fat with half-notes
from the Cracker song, playing somewhere
for the third time, but I hear
Moon River and Bad Moon Rising,
or Once in a Blue Moon and laugh
straight up as far as I can see,
stepping back to watch it,
until something hard jams me down—
a fist, a fence—it doesn't
really matter. I can wedge my mouth
against the chain links and scream
at the couples grinding against
their car doors, but after midnight,
we all need help. The dirt is cold.
The clearest things I see are light-years
away. I can find the Seven Sisters but
I know they're just a part of Taurus,
I know these things. I know so many
useless things, like blood looks black
in the moonlight, and hanging on
the wire I think, I'm only one
more person, and it's only one
hour into Sunday, and I think
if that balloon doesn't come back
right now, and show me how it's done,
I'll never make it out. By God,
I'll never find my way again.

When Cowboys Cry

by Judy Blunt

In a nearly shadowed corner
beyond his mother's open
coffin, just a dozen running
steps from the calm ranks

of flower carts and mostly
empty folding chairs, the whole
of my father's face simply turned
and came apart, like an old wall

falls one hard brick at a time.
And the whispering all stopped
and the little girls crossed
their new Mary Janes and watched

the new empty place this all
left behind, and the mourners
stared hard at the mother's
sealed eyes, and the men read

their hats for signs—like nothing
solid can grow on soft ground
or things usually heal best
when they're left alone—so no one

meddled until it all come together
and the mother was wheeled away
with her flowers and the gunmetal
chairs were paired neatly and put

aside and my father took his place
in the first pew and gave his mother
away with good solid grace and shook
hands with everybody after. Later

at the big supper they all said
they thought the better of him
for a few tears, and if not here
for chrissake, among friends, then where?

Laurie Wagner Buyer

I WAS NOT BORN TO THE LAND. I came West in 1975 from Chicago with a backpack and twenty-five dollars in cash. I thought I would stay one winter and I ended up staying for life. From the outset, it was never easy. The rudimentary skills of a homestead lifestyle, from splitting wood and carrying water to birthing and butchering, came hard for me. But I did learn, and my love for the land flourished easily.

There is purpose to life here. It's part of an eternal cycle. Because the animals become, in great portion, your reason for getting up every morning (they rely solely on you for their feed and care), they become very important—not only because they provide the dollars necessary to keep on ranching, but because they become part of you. My husband's grandfather once told him, "you don't own those cows, they own you." If I didn't have a connection to the land and the animals, I wouldn't have a life . . . and I was extremely fortunate to find a man, a kindred spirit, to share it all with me.

Gathering Mint
by Laurie Wagner Buyer

He woke quiet, ate potatoes and eggs
sitting alone on a cottonwood stump in the sun.

At noon he took a rifle, burlap bag, and handful
   of dried apples,
saddled the glass-eyed gelding, corralled
   the wayward mare,
whistled one long high note for the hound
   and was gone.

It was late the first summer, river running
   low, meadow grass tassels paled by wind.
I weeded the garden one faded row at a time
   while the goats lazed in barn shade
and the mare paced,
   nickering again and again.

He returned at dusk, drunk on solitude, singing
   in time with the gelding's rocky trot,
moccasined feet wet with mud,
   the burlap bag he tossed me
stuffed full of mint
   from the beaver slough.

Purple Tulips

by Laurie Wagner Buyer

for Kathy and Roz

After a weekend of Shakespeare
and talk and friends, the renewal of
feminine joys long since left by the way,
traffic pours into Denver as I alone turn
west into the mountains heading home.

Kenosha rises in still-life splendor:
dark pines melded into darker skies,
billowing thunderheads pierced by
sun streams and a fleeting, startling
streak of bluest summer blue.

Whatever did we talk of ten hours
straight while we laughed and ate,
women cuddled in conversation,
finding comfort and a sheltered kind
of peace while it thundered and rained.

Home to me is a man and a dog waiting
by the gate. The simplest welcome
draws me into his embrace. He'll never
know of Eudora Welty or Anais Nin yet I
find wonder in our companionable silences.

Playing hard to catch, my sorrel hunkers
stockstill deep in the willow bottom
never knowing that his blaze face betrays him;
he's savvy, canny, holds his breath when
I jerk tight the cinch slack, strap on spurs.

Acceptance is a part of age. How relaxing
finally to be able to giggle like girls at
ourselves, our men, our lives, the unfathomable,
intangible marks that brand each of our days
and nights as decidedly different, especial.

Riding to cattle he talks of grass and
sky and water, weight gain and culls,
whether to cut the hay this year or leave
it stand, thigh high and heavy headed,
waving amber tassels in the August wind.

Director of Development. Vice Principal.
I cannot seem to imagine your lives beyond
the executive titles as I unsaddle and stomp,
easing the ache in my knees. Ranch wife is
life to me now despite my city beginnings.

We've each worked so long to be where we are:
centered, happy. Never lost now, occasionally
wandering, wondering how to follow the myriad
directions of the heart that lead us further
and further apart from what we thought we'd be.

Before first light the black crowned night
heron cries and cries . . . it will be all right
if we just remember to turn left at the purple
tulips, look for the sun's shadow on the edge
of the road; it'll always bring us home.

Eight Rabbits
by Laurie Wagner Buyer

Eight rabbits hang skinned in pale spring sun. Old
dog gnaws patiently the severed heads, velvet ears.

In autumn I found his scrawled note, the rifle
missing. I was alone when the bloodhounds came.

Men swarmed through the woods, the hounds bayed low,
unsure. You rode through the dark hours searching.

By the corral, the orphaned colt sucking my fingers, I
knew the outcome. Bloodhounds won't go near a dead man.

Nothing to say, the silent months fade past. Still you watch,
questioning everything, even my rabbits, cold in the sunshine.

Flowering Almond

by Jane Candia Coleman

for Edith

You feed the turtles cat food
at four o'clock each afternoon,
let skunks nest behind old doors
on your porch; the bright-eyed babies
tumble at your feet each night
flashing black fur and wilderness.

Today you take me into your garden
of staked plants, oxalis burning at the gate,
and into your square plains house
with helter-skelter rooms, tables buried
under photographs and doilies, letters,
plants, nuts and colored stones, a Bible
and a spool with scarlet thread meandering.

You offer me a pear,
green-gold in a curving dish,
so ripe the juice spills down my chin
like honey-water, and I lick it,
sweeping the last goodness with my tongue
while I read your diaries,
sixty years of valley history recalled . . .

> *The white leghorns laid today. First time.*
> *The eggs were fine.*
> *Went up the creek, cut wood, drove the wagon down.*
> *Bought 18 dozen clothespins at the store.*
> *The baby died. Ground so hard we dug all day.*
> *The paint mare foaled a brown stud colt.*
> *My almond tree put out a flower.*
> *Two dry years and cattle dropping.*
> *I lug water to the tree and pray . . .*

What lies in my lap is the coming and going
of lives and seasons; a ritual,
as the twilight whirling of wild babies,
as the branch of your almond tree
laid lightly down along the split rail fence
each spring for years.

Jane Candia Coleman

I WAS BORN IN THE WRONG PLACE —Pittsburgh, Pennsylvania— and knew it by age four. Fortunately I lived in the country, and by the time I was eight I knew every farmer, every horse owner for miles around. But somewhere, somehow, I knew I'd end up in the West and dedicated myself to learning about it.

When I finally got to Arizona for the first time, I didn't feel that I was a stranger. Instead of being daunted by the long vistas, the hugeness of the land, I remember quite plainly that I thought, "Why, I can grow as big as I want, as is possible, and no one will tell me I can't." During the next years I spent as much time as possible out here. I took oral histories, studied the plants and animals, rode the high deserts and the mountains. When, in 1986, I ended an abusive marriage, I got in my car and, as did so many others before me, headed West toward a new life. I ended up on my own ranch with a new—and very supportive—husband, five horses, five dogs, and five cats.

Old Pete
by Jane Candia Coleman

First light. The old mule
leans against your door
and heaves and coughs,
nose in the dust.

You know what you have to do,
except you never thought
he would follow so easy,
come behind you through new grass
like a hound.

Thirty years is a long time
to be together.
Marriage of a kind.
You touch him—
shoulder and gaunt flank—
but you don't say "So Long"
lest he hear
and raise his head.

You leave him where he falls
for coyotes that will feast
this night. And you think
walking back across the pasture,
it takes forever to get home.

Poor Will's Widow
by Jane Candia Coleman

Broad-faced as a cow, with bony knees
and elbows jutting out like fence posts,
you sit, unlikely sinner, in the Sears chair
with the purple throw, sorting peaches while we talk.

I remind myself you are an adulteress,
a fallen woman who moved right in
on Charley and his twenty cats
and loved them all for years.

I ask, wasn't it lonely
back in those mountains,
shunned by the righteous,
by all the wives on market day?

Wasn't it more penance than paradise,
with neither of you young,
fighting the dry years, those cats so wild
they weighed the table down, mealtimes?

You shift, a sack of angles,
neither lush nor schooled in love.
Lonely? No. No time for that,
though Charley never talked a lot.

Those hills were full of talk—
turkeys gobbling, coyotes hunting
down the wash,
and Lord knows, jays are never still.

And all night in summer
the poor-wills calling just like folks.
Poor-will . . . poor-will . . .
In bed you'd hear them
a lullaby strung out till dawn.

Poor-will . . . poor-will . . .
Two notes. Enough for birds
to make a life.
Enough for a smart woman
who, when a man cares,
don't need a heap of words
to prove it.

Sandhill Cranes

by Jane Candia Coleman

We sit on the orange-striped couch,
the old woman in a purple dress,
her face a land of gullies, seams, erosions.

It's not the bowl I bargain for that's important.
What I need is the comfort of women talking,
the sound of words that matter.
What I want is forgiveness
for coming with dollars
to buy the spirit of her grandmother
walled in clay.

I tell her I have seen blackbirds
nesting in the cottonwoods,
heard the call of frogs
from the ruins by the river.
And she tells me the cranes flew over
crying long in the moonlight.

Now we are at ease with one another,
wrapped in the music of migrating birds,
in the spirit of the grandmother
who in her bowl left one line broken—
an open door she passes through.

Peggy Simson Curry

O NE SUMMER WHEN I WAS thirteen years old, I rode out after supper at the ranch. I rode along the edge of the meadow to the head of a place called the Grand Draw, a canyon. While I was there the whole area illuminated. It was the strangest experience, out of the blue. I thought, *This is a part of the creative world . . . I love the world of nature.*

If we are creative people, what happens to us is never enough; we are impelled to capture what we know in the ultimate reality of artistic pattern. Writing is a way of life. At best it is a rewarding combination of creative experience and creative expression. One cannot exist without the other. Memorable writing can happen only out of memorable living. I write to find out just who the hell I am.

(Peggy Simson Curry died in 1987.)

When Words First Spoke to Me
by Peggy Simson Curry

When words first spoke to me—
not out of human mouths
or from the winds
or tasseled in the webs
of spiders spinning sun—
when words first spoke to me
as living symbols of myself
there were three books: HOLY BIBLE
POETRY OF ROBERT BURNS DISEASES OF CATTLE.

Library in ranch wilderness
thirty miles from town,
many months deserted to dust and flies.
More often we read the sky's
templed ultimatums of spring,
omens of snow,
portents of hail and rain.
Wind scribbled messages on clouds,
vowels came howling out of canyons,
consonants lisped through clumps of grass.

By lamplight my father read "Tam o Shanter"
voice rich with dialect burr
while mother embroidered flannel
that I might sleep
with bluebells on my sleeves.

One day she gave away the Bible,
presented it to neighbor-trapper—
rude gust from carcasses and creeks—
that God and cleanliness might work together
purifying him who praised her oatcakes
and her tea. Sent him home with Book
bandaged in clean white towel,
passages underlined to help him into Heaven.

When words first spoke to me
the rain was falling.
In dusky afternoon I opened heavy book,
DISEASES OF CATTLE, turned pages
where small words danced like flies
on screen doors sultry nights before supper.
Two words rose up, looming large as mountain
peaks beyond the meadows—HEMORRHAGIC SEP-
TICEMIA!

Father! Father in the woodshed chopping wood
tell me, tell me what they say!

A song of crickets and silver then,
a sound of bees and moaning,
a sadness of sick and bleeding cattle
told from tiny mouths of letters.

Fevers   furies   fascination
crystals in the ear
bluebells ringing
strokes of wonder on the tongue
to say again   again
hemorrhagic septicemia   hemorrhagic septicemia.

The Hunt
by Peggy Simson Curry

High country, man's country in October, hunter's acres
That smell of animal heat—wild breath of buck,
Raw scent of urine on the fallen leaf.
By lantern light we fondle rifles into scabbards,
Ride out across dark meadows, Big Dipper hung
Like a Holy Grail in the cold north sky.

We hide our horses on an aspen-covered slope,
Settle like the fox among the sagebrush.
In first thin light the naked willows hang
Like wavering smoke along the creek below.
Wind rises gently as a woman out of sleep,
Carries scent of mud-banked beaver ponds.

A great buck drifts from his willow shelter;
His branched head holds the morning up.
In slow procession three does follow him to drink.
When he climbs the slope he walks as though he owned
The world and all the world's beginnings. And I
Lay my rifle down before majesty so wild and pure.

Silver-blue and cold the barrel of my father's gun
Rises out of sagebrush. The shot shatters the morning.
Thunder echoes down the valley, dies among the hills.
The great buck climbs the sky, hoofs paw at crimson clouds.
He hangs a moment there, as though he sought some passage
To a star, then his legs fold up like broken sticks,
His antlers dig the dust, plow up the sagebrush.
The does descend in terror to the waiting willows.

I follow my father down the slope, watch him
Cut the still-warm throat, see small sunrise
Burst around my feet, sink to darkness in the earth,
Leave bubbles like last surf of heat's red sea.
From slashed belly, hide and skin curl back
And entrails tumble out in glistening silver loops—
Steaming fruits of life soon harvested by flies.

They hang the buck from somber pine, the raw
And empty belly braced apart to cool in shade
And rising wind of morning. I close my eyes
And see him walk again from darkness into light,
The great head lifted toward the sky.
When I look again upon the world, blinded by the sun,
I have grown old beyond my years. My ears fill
With prophecies a coyote wails across the barren ridges,
Prophecies of all things lost—lost and never found again.

Jack Patton
by Peggy Simson Curry

Jack Patton, Commander of rakers in the hay field,
Jack Patton, General of my thirteenth summer,
Jack Patton cursing me on hot afternoons when I
stop to gulp tepid water from a canvas bag.
Jack Patton scolding me to make another round
while others leave the field, making me drive
the old gray team until I scream in tears and rage.

"If you do it, do it right," he says.

Stuck it out all summer, face burned black,
behind numb from rake seat, arms stiff tugging lines,
stuck it out too tired to eat at noon, too tired
to wash for supper, stuck it out and hated him.

"If you do it, do it right," he said.

Wished him all manner of evil:
Lord, give him loose bowels squatting in a ditch
before the President of the United States.
Lord, make him have pimples on his face the size of horse turds.
Lord, let his penis fall off, be eaten by a million flies.

All my life remembering, "If you do it, do it right."

Cowpath
by Ruth Daniels

I walk slower . . .
steps more uncertain
as I follow the cowpath
down past the spring
to the sandy creek bed.

The pecans Grandpa planted
have their roots sunk deep.
A gunny sack of rich brown nuts
once bought a black taffeta dress
that whispered when I sashayed.

The trail goes by
the blackberry thicket
where a briar still reaches
for a careless knee . . .
I linger and my tongue
remembers the pleasure
of eating sun warmed fruit.

I can hear
Bessie's bell on the evening breeze
and see Duke's yellow tail
waving over the pasture grass
as he comes back panting
from a rabbit chase.

A shadow crosses the sun.
It's been fifty years
since Bessie and Duke.
I am old and walk
with uncertain steps
back on the path
to where the farmhouse stood.

I'M THE THIRD GENERATION ON THE family farm in Oklahoma. We were displaced during the dust-bowl depression era but managed to hold on to the land. I married and raised my family living in an urban area, but my roots and values have always come from the young rural upbringing. We returned to the farm twenty-one years ago. I'm retired now, sixty-seven years old, living close to the land and loving every old rock and gully.

City Cousin
by Ruth Daniels

In her twentieth summer
she came to the farm for a visit.
At ten I thought her as glamorous
as any movie star.
A slender girl,
sparkling as a spring day,
a cap of black hair
cut in wind-blown bob,
spit curls clinging to a creamy cheek.
Her boy-friend brought her . . .
a patrolman on the police force,
tailor-made uniform, gun on hip.

As usual Mother did the weekly wash,
sprinkling it down in a bushel basket.
Flat irons heated on the kitchen wood stove.
I ironed the pillow cases,
handkerchiefs, cotton slips,
and my hair ribbons.

I shook out a piece
of pretty peach material,
darker lace on top and bottom.
Mama said, "For heaven's sake
be careful."
The iron glided like skating on ice,
her perfume mingling with the steam.

I ironed that satin slip,
the first I'd ever seen,
making myself a promise . . .
One day I would have one
to shape my hoped-for bosom,
cling to my thighs like a silky skin,
rustle around my legs
when I stepped out
into the grown-up world.

Lyn DeNaeyer

I'M A THIRD-GENERATION RANCHER in the Sandhills of Nebraska, on a place which was homesteaded by my grandparents in 1889. I've been actively involved in ranching all my life, but increasingly so since the death of my husband and my father. Right now, I'm running the operation in partnership with my mother and my son. It's a typical cow-calf deal, and every effort is made to incorporate environmentally sound practices in the fragile ecosystem of the Sandhills, while retaining the common-sense approach which made it possible to hang onto the land thus far. I recently returned to school to complete a degree in Mental Health and Counseling. I hope I can combine that career with ranching and still find time to write.

Reflection
by Lyn DeNaeyer

It was open session sign up
When she arrived with him in tow
And he wanted her to enter,
Join him singin' in the show,
But she refused to hear of it
'Cause this would be his day to shine.
Besides, she'd have all she could do
To keep the damned old coot in line.

Y' see, he's just a mite eccentric
And folks avoid him in our town
Or make a cruel joke of him
When they're sure he's not around.
He rides uptown on a mangy hoss
And wears an American flag
Stuck in the crown of his battered hat,
And gravy stained britches that bag.

But today he's half presentable,
Got his Sunday manners on.
I'm relieved he's trackin' clearly;
Some days his mind is near 'bout gone.
The committee saw this comin'
And they've commissioned me MC
Of this load of trouble that we've bought
And on this we all agree,

When on the stage we set him loose
No one else will get a chance
To tell a poem or sing a song
Of cowboy humor and romance.
Of wrangler days and hobo ways
And countless other things he'll tell.
He's long winded and unruly,
He'll no doubt cuss a bit as well.

But I call each one on stage in turn;
He sings a song of cowboy lore
In a voice truer than expected
For a man of eighty years and more.
Soon I'm breathin' somewhat easier;
We've made it through another round.
When he's invited up again
To my surprise, he turns it down.

Can't think of one right now, he says,
And as we move on with the show
I watch him out there practicin'.
Then he gets up, kinda slow
And as he performs the last time
Down in the center front I see
Something no one else can notice
And it's a message meant for me.

His gaze is fastened on her face
And she's cuein' him each line.
The pride's apparent in her eyes
And tears are wellin' up in mine
'Cause right now I'm lookin' inward
And not so proud of what I see.
I've just witnessed something priceless.
You can't buy love like that, it's free.

While we've all spun our tales of dreams,
Mine have been cut down to size
For I've not been privileged to see
That look of care in someone's eyes.
And as self appointed critics
We're all in need of some correction
'Cause the measure of God's creatures
Is always found in love's reflection.

Breakin' Even
by Lyn DeNaeyer

He might sit on the steps of an evenin'
And watch the kids cruisin' Main,
While she wonders how they came to this
And how long he can stand the strain
Of never havin' room to breathe
And the mem'ries burnin' his brain.

"Son, you know a cowman don't get rich,"
Is what his daddy would say,
"But if a man can just break even
He'll always be able to stay
And he won't have to answer to no one
But his God at the end of the day."

So he walked in his old man's footprints
And he's never been nothin' but glad
That his daddy and grand-dad gave him
A chance at the life that they had.
But sometimes he can't help blamin' himself
For the way that it's turned out so bad.

He knows it's not like the old times
And folks have got pretty strange.
Breakin' even won't cut it these days
And the rules; well, they seemed to change.
Some fellers that don't know one end of a cow
From another control all the range.

Here lately, she's been noticin'
More grey in his hair than brown,
Ever since the day they rented this place
When the P.C.A. was shut down
And they moved the kids and the gooseneck
And the old blue heeler to town.

She's got a job at the diner,
And he's working by the day
And sometimes at the auction barn.
He doesn't brag much on the pay
But it's keepin' the rust off of his spurs
And the sorrel mare gets her hay.

When he mentions he drove by the home place
She knows that he isn't done grievin'.
He's still packin' up the mem'ries
Left over from their leavin'.
She's just prayin' they'll get him by
Till the day his heart breaks even.

Elizabeth Ebert

I WAS BORN OF POOR BUT HONEST parents"—actually, we weren't just poor, we were poverty-stricken like most of the South Dakotans in the '30s. But we always managed to have books and read aloud a lot. Mother was a quoter and reciter and Dad was a natural-born storyteller. I have loved western stories ever since Mother read "Covered Wagon" when I was six. I suppose I was a sort of solitary child as I was two years younger than most of my classmates and loved school and books. My favorite poets were Badger Clark, Dorothy Parker, and Tennyson—now there is a weird trio! I guess I am rather drawn to the long, sad stories . . . though I do not consider myself a sad person. Life is not easy for small ranchers, but I would not want to be anything else.

Store Candy
by Elizabeth Ebert

"Don't go," she said, "We'll do with what we have."
    She knew her words would be to no avail,
He never understood her strange, fey fears
    Of spectral things that lurked beside the trail.
She'd seen them in the storm the night before
    And though the wind had hushed now and the snow
No longer slid in sibilant whispers, still she knew
    That they were waiting. "Please don't go!"

"The weather'll hold," he said. "Our son will have
    Store candy in his stocking Christmas morn,
And we'll keep Christmas as it should be kept.
    Santa must ride." He left her there forlorn.
She watched the horse and rider disappear,
    Her nervous fingers plucked her apron fold.
The whistled notes of "Jingle Bells" came back
    Like icy echoes in the still, clear cold.

All day she worked as though she were possessed.
    She nursed the babe and saw their son was fed;
She scrubbed and polished 'til the cabin shone,
    She baked the pies, and mixed the Christmas bread,
And hung the decorations on the tree—
    Small crafted things tied on with bright yarn strands;
And to their son's delight she sat and cut
    Long chains of paper angels holding hands.

The sundogs danced the weary sun to rest,
    She lit the lamp and still he wasn't there.
She hung the stockings up beside the fire,
    And tucked the children in and said a prayer.
Then she waited, watching by the window,
    The eerie lights were flaring all across the sky,
And she waited, listening, only hearing
    The old clock tick the anxious minutes by.

He rode the trail, hunched up against the cold,
    Intent on reaching home before the night,
His saddlebags bulged out like Santa's pack.
    He did not see the shadow, white on white,
That sat upon the bank. The long ears twitched,
    The haunches crouched to spring in quick retreat.
The snow crust broke. The frightened rabbit slid
    Flailing in terror, beneath the horse's feet.

The startled horse lashed out. He slipped and fell.
    He rose to run and crashed into a tree.
The low-hung branches caught the rider hard,
    The saddle turned, the man did not fall free
But, foot through stirrup, in cold, stiff leather hung,
    Unconscious and unknowing from the shock,
He dragged behind that frantic, headlong flight
    Across the iron-hard waste of brush and rock
Until at last the horse steadied himself,
    Retraced his way back to the trail to stand
Head down and patient, waiting for the man
    To rise and mount again and take command.

The blood pooled red and froze upon the snow,
    The man moved not nor did he draw a breath.
Night shadows crept across the quiet hills,
    Then there was only darkness, cold and death.
A coyote cried from up along the ridge,
    The horse pawed nervously, began to take
Slow, sidewise steps down that long trail toward home,
    Dragging the inert body in his wake.

She heard them coming down along the trail,
    She grabbed her coat and lantern and she flew
Outside to meet him, holding high the light.
    She looked but once, and then she knew—she knew
That he was far beyond her power to aid,
    There was no one on earth could help him now
And she alone must do what must be done.
    She could not leave the children anyhow;

Nor could she bring that broken thing inside;
    For their small sakes she must keep Christmas Day;
And so she dragged him down into a stall
    And laid him gently on a pile of hay,
Then slipping back into the house, she knelt,
    Drew from its hiding place beneath their bed
Her Christmas gift to him, a patchwork quilt
    She'd sewn in secret and she'd tied in red
Because he liked bright colors. She covered him,
    Smoothed the quilt carefully, and as she turned to go,
She stumbled on one snowy saddlebag.
    She opened it, with fingers still and slow

And gazed upon the sacks of Christmas sweets.
    The lantern flared and flickered, and it seemed
The shadows drew in closer, taunted her,
    Reached boldly out to grasp her, and she screamed
And screamed; and in blind terror took the candy
    By the handsful, the gaudy green and red,
And threw it at those dancing shapes until
    The saddlebag was empty. Then she fled
Into the house and shut and locked the door
    And leaned against it, too spent to even cry;
Stared vaguely 'round the room until
    Those two small empty stockings caught her eye.

She slowly filled them up with homemade sweets
    And little gifts, then sat there cold and numb
Until their son awoke with joyous cries
    That Santa Claus had really, truly come.

And she kept Christmas, all that endless day,
    And all the next, 'til punchers riding back
From holiday carousal in the town
    Read out the story written in the track.
They saw the hat, the broken branch, the blood,
    And followed that grim trail until they found
The battered corpse beneath the patchwork quilt
    And all the bright store candy scattered round.

An Ordinary Morning
by Elizabeth Ebert

'Twas just an ordinary mornin'
    Somewhere along in May
When my husband hollered from the yard,
    And then I heard him say,
"I'm going to the pasture.
    It'll take an hour or two,
And if you'd like to come along,
    We'll drive out in Old Blue."

Now I don't get to tag along
    Much, as a general rule,
But I'd finished with the chorin'
    And the kids were all in school.
'Twould be just like we were courtin.'
    I was happy for the chance,
Cause you take it where you find it
    When it comes to ranch romance.

Now Old Blue is kind of ancient
    And he's got some scars and dents
'Cause we use him when we're feedin'
    Checkin' cows and fixin' fence,
But the engine runs like clockwork,
    And the tires are pretty fair,
All except that right front whitewall
    That sometimes loses air,

And there's a chunk of balin' wire
    To fasten down the hood,
And a saddle blanket for the seat
    Where the cushion's not too good.
The cab is kind of cluttered up
    With stuff we need, that's true,
There's vet supplies and fencin' tools,
    And ropes and rifles too.

Well, we headed for the pasture.
    (Course I opened every gate.)
And we found that little heifer,
    The one that calved so late.
Her bag was near to bustin',
    Milk was drippin' from each teat,
For she'd kick that little feller
    Every time he tried to eat.

So my husband said, "I'll fix her,
    And I'll do it slick as soap,
'Cause I've got you here to help me
    And I brought along my rope.
Now I'll ride Blue on the fender
    And you steer him from the seat,
And I'll rope that little mama
    And we'll let her baby eat."

Well, I lined up on that heifer,
    And he built himself a loop.
Then she took off at a gallop,
    So I just poured on the soup
And Old Blue was doin' thirty
    When we topped that little knoll,
But he had her caught for certain—
    Then I hit that badger hole!

The cow kept right on goin'
    But we made a sudden stop.
My husband landed underneath
    And Old Blue was there on top,
But I saw that rope come trailin' by
    And it cheered me up a mite,
So I jumped right out and grabbed it,
    And I snubbed that critter tight

Around a most convenient rock.
　　You should have heard her beller!
Then I went a lookin' for the calf,
　　And I brought that little feller
And I held him to his mama,
　　And it really pleased me some
To see that little belly
　　Growin' round just like a drum.

Made me think about my husband—
　　So I went back to Old Blue
To kind of take a look around,
　　See what I had to do.
Blue was standin' kind of hip-slung
　　'Cause one wheel was up some higher,
But it wasn't nothin' I couldn't fix
　　With just some balin' wire.

My husband lay there underneath,
　　Said he thought his leg was broke,
But it made me pretty happy
　　Just to know he didn't croak.
Well I twisted stuff together
　　And I stuck Blue in reverse,
And I backed out of that badger hole.
　　Then I heard my husband curse;

And when I stopped to think of it,
　　He was right, without a doubt,
Instead of backin' over him,
　　I should have pulled him out.
Well, I got him loaded in Old Blue
　　'Mongst all those other things,
Propped his leg up with that blanket,
　　Though it meant I rode the springs.

And we finally limped on into town,
　　Not travelin' very fast.
Old Blue, he got new tie-rods,
　　And my husband got a cast.
Just an ordinary mornin',
　　Really nothin' out of line . . .
By the way, I checked that heifer,
　　And the calf is doin' fine.

Song From The Day the Pump Broke
by Elizabeth Ebert

We fought the water pipes all day,
Or rather he did, while I held the tools
And cooked him steak for lunch, and hoped
My presence at his side would comfort bring.
We needed water soon, the stock must drink;
But nothing seemed to work. 'Twas dusk
Before we found which parts should be replaced.
I drove the thirty miles to town
Because his eye ached and his shoulders too.

I watched him through the dusty plumber's glass:
The mud-caked jeans, unshaven face,
The squinting eye. He looked so very tired
—and *old!* My heart caught in my throat
And through the quick hot tears I saw
My life's one verity, the pivot point
On which my world revolves:
I love you, and I always will, my dear.

Gretel Ehrlich

The Orchard
by Gretel Ehrlich

We go into it at night.
In Wyoming an orchard is the
only city around—so many blossoms going up
into trees like lights
and windfall apples like lives
coming down.

In the pickup, heads on the tailgate,
we lie on last year's hay and wait
for the orchard to bloom.
A great horned owl sweeps between
trees as if to cropdust the rising
sap with white for the flowers.

"The first blossom to come," you say,
"I'll give the apple that grows there to you."

Another owl lands
on a bare branch and drops
a plug of micebones to the roots.
Under him, the tree does not think of
the sap's struggle.
I listen to your heart. Divided by
beats and rests, it says yes, then no, then yes.

Above us the Milky Way seams the sky and is
stirred by a hand too big to see.
We watch the stars.

Tonight so many of them fall.

I CAME TO WYOMING IN 1976. I had not planned to stay, but I couldn't make myself leave. John, the sheepman, put me to work immediately. It was spring, and shearing time. For fourteen days of fourteen hours each, we moved thousands of sheep through sorting corrals to be sheared, branded, and deloused. I suspect that my original motive for coming here was to "lose myself" in new and unpopulated territory. Instead of producing the numbness I thought I wanted, life on the sheep ranch woke me up. The vitality of the people I was working with flushed out what had become a hallucinatory rawness inside me. I threw away my clothes and bought new ones; I cut my hair. The arid country was a clean slate. Its absolute indifference steadied me.

For David

by Gretel Ehrlich

"What happens to people that love each other?"
"I suppose they have whatever they have and they are more
fortunate than others. Then one gets the emptiness forever."
    —Ernest Hemingway; ACROSS THE RIVER AND INTO THE TREES

I.

Then we feed the cattle with
a sorrel team and a sled.
We break bales like bread
and scatter them before the wind.
Sometimes we cross the river
on bad ice to check for calves because
one cow backed up to a wash and
dropped her calf into the water.
And after, empty and light with no load,
we bump home across snowy furrows.

I dream we pull you
through all the seasons: through autumn's
hot temper when trees are
moods and the sky is
charcoaled black then whitestruck
until May. Then we are not
breaking bales but lives and they
are scattered bones in a crossing wind.

Sometimes I can't unharness you.
Your death is a horse.
I can't unwrap from my wrists these
leather lines that tie us together.
Then you lie in my lungs and
break words across my breath like water.
You tell me anything I can hear.

II.

Once when a surgeon said
your chances of making it were "pie in the sky,"
a mask of weather lowered over us.
I asked, "Ether or oxygen?" But the mask
just came down. That day broke you.
And when the clock unwound you said,
"Let's not tell time anymore."

III.

Now I have to learn words that say
the complication of who you were.
Memory breaks open its head and
throws you too far, then slams you close:
Eyes. Voice. Hands. Scar.
And the wind blows death into your black hair.

IV.

They buried your ashes and planted
a tree in them. Sometimes a wind
comes and shapes grass into
little bayonets as if protecting your absence.
And the tree, like the surgeon's needle,
punctures me with its spinal, bending song
until all the air is gone
from words and the emptiness I feel
is forever.

Born in the Afternoon

by Gretel Ehrlich
    for Victress Hitchcock

Against barbed wire an antelope
gives birth by the road. It's all sage here.
I drive through rings and rings of mountains.
The radio says: rain mixed with snow in the
southeast tonight: a traveler's advisory:
the mountain passes are slick.
In front of me a raincloud crowns the sky in
your direction, Vickie, where you're
breathing and birthing. Remember to stay in the moment
with the pain. Let this cloud draw rain
through your body to soothe and clean,
to nourish the child who's been growing there.
Right now earth gives two messages:
a female duck flies over the car:
the stub of a rainbow shoots up from
a ridge and disappears in clouds.
Child, Child, still unnamed, unsexed,
let go of your sleek garden of water,
lower yourself through the locks of your mother's body,
climb down this wet ladder of weather—
rain to earth—and wake up
on a pillow of sage where
antelope, too, are born in the afternoon.

Happy Birthday
by Martha Downer Ellis

One afternoon while I was over in the office
Working on the registered cow records
Abel came in—
Happy birthday, Mrs. Ellis.
It wasn't my birthday, but I thought
Maybe it was his, so I said,
Happy birthday, Abel.

Reaching in his levi pocket he said,
I don't know when is your birthday,
But some day is your birthday—
And handed me three perfect
Little bird points
He had found over by Gavilán.

Martha Downer Ellis

MY HUSBAND, GEORGE F. Ellis, was manager of the Bell Ranch in northeastern New Mexico for twenty-six years, and I lived at Headquarters longer than any woman ever had. I have always been immersed in the beauty and majesty of the area's vast open spaces and of the big blue sky over and around me. I am fascinated by this beauty and by the thoughts, feelings and actions of all of us God has chosen to inhabit it. I try to encompass these in my poetry.

Never Let Us Think
by Martha Downer Ellis

Never let us think that Waddingham or Montoya
Was the first to live along La Cinta's water.
Comanche, Kiowa, and Apache,
Clovis man, and Folsom, came before.

Never let us think they were the first
To pull the earth up around them
For shelter of stone or adobe or brick.

Never let us think they were the first
To taste the flesh of game
That grazed the Seco grass.

Never let us think they were the first
To see the rain come sweeping over the River
Or a rainbow shine on Gavilán.

Never let us think that we shall be the last.

People Will Talk
by June Brander Gilman

You may get thru the world, but it'll be very slow
If you listen to all that is said as you go;
You'll be worried and fretted, and kept in a stew,
As meddlesome tongues must have something to do,
    For people will talk!

If you're quiet and modest, you'll have it presumed
That your humble position is only assumed,
You're a wolf in sheep's clothing, or else you're a fool;
But don't get excited, keep perfectly cool,
    For people will talk!

And then if you show the least boldness of heart,
Or a slight inclination to take your own part,
They'll call you an upstart, conceited and vain;
But keep straight ahead, don't stop to explain,
    For people will talk!

If threadbare your shirt or old-fashioned your hat,
Someone will surely take notice of that
And hint very strongly you can't pay your way;
But mind your own business, whatever they say,
    For people will talk!

If your clothes are in fashion, don't think to escape,
for they criticize then in a different shape,
You're ahead of your means, your tailor's unpaid;
But pay them no heed; there's naught to be made,
    For people will talk!

Now, the best way to do is to do as you please,
For your mind, at least, will then be at ease;
Of course, you will meet with all sorts of abuse,
But don't think to stop them, it's not any use,
    For people will talk!

June Brander Gilman
Helen Kay Brander

MY SISTER KAY AND I GREW up on a pioneer homestead in Montana. Times were hard and we went to live with our older sisters, who were rodeo performers. To earn money, we rode for neighboring ranches, gave rodeos, worked in the hay fields, and logged in the winter. Kay eventually married and later became a well-known newspaperwoman in Colorado; my husband and I bought a ranch in Montana, which he ran while I worked for a mining company and helped on the weekends. Both Kay and I wrote poetry, but this is the only poem we ever collaborated on. She died of cancer in 1981.

My husband died in 1973 and I've run the ranch since then. I have just finished my haying for this year and am now back to irrigating. It has been a bad season, what with rain every other day or so. Since I do all my own work except running the bale wagon, it's a slow process. I am now 76 and not getting any faster, but then I have all the rest of my life to get the work done.

Peggy Godfrey

MY HUSBAND WORKS FOR A construction company while I run a sheep and cow-calf operation near Moffat, Colorado. In the summer I do contract haying and hire out as a hand on the Double Bar V Ranch at the north end of the San Luis Valley, one of the highest and most severe ranchlands in the world. I like the seasonal variations of this life, its silence and solitude as well as the sometimes hectic pace. It's a *see, hear, touch, smell, taste* sort of life, something that lends itself to being savored.

When my second baby (my only girl) was stillborn, I learned that loss qualifies something as firmly as gain does. Though it is hard to explain this, grief gave me a certain capacity for my work that I hadn't had before—more awareness, a deeper trust in intuition, a gift for calving and lambing with techniques and reverence that I really don't understand. The experiences of my country life provided me with the resilience to give it my best and recognize the value of even the hard times.

Old Vogal
by Peggy Godfrey

Told me I was lucky
When I went to cut his hay
A bloom or two means lots of leaves
'Course it's best that way.

He assured me I was lucky
That my bales were done up tight
Lucky that I caught the dew
And chanced to bale it right.

Oh yes, and I was lucky
When storm clouds came around
All my hay was in a stack
Not layin' on the ground.

I clenched my jaw and held my tongue
Red anger 'round me swirled
If I was a man, he'd say I was good,
But "lucky" 'cuz I'm a girl.

Roland
by Peggy Godfrey

Everyone was sure
Roland was my pa.
It never seemed the bond we shared
Was daughter and father-in-law.

Adaptable, inventive
His mechanic expertise
With Roland for a teacher
New skills came with ease.

I learned to drive a pickup truck
In mud and snow and slush,
Learned to pull a trailer
Stacked with hay or logs or brush.

He taught me how to tie down loads
With come-along and chain
How to use a cheater
On all the heavy things.

I recall my apprehension
Backing trailer-loads of hay:
Through the gate, then square the load
There is no easy way.

He walked me through the basics
Of coolant, oil, and grease,
Battery, belts, and hoses,
How to find and fix the leaks.

I never saw him panic
Or cater to despair
He'd manage every problem
And face it shoulders square.

The only dream I ever had
To wake me up in tears—
It kept me in distress for days
And tender all these years.

I dreamed I found my dear friend slumped
Across a bale of hay
He had no breath, no heartbeat
So still in death he lay.

The light of day denied the death
That shadowed last night's sleep
His health and strength were evidence
I had no cause to weep.

But deep within this woman
Lurked some childish fears
Untouched subtle messages
From her early years:

"Strength and power are man's domain
A man can choose his path
His work, his happiness come first—
A woman gets what's left.

An independent woman is a curse
She weakens man.
He who gives his power away
By teaching her is damned."

Not understanding how dreams heal
Nor how they set us free
I felt, as I grew stronger,
His death was caused by me.

In simple desperation
My heart within me wrenched:
I wanted to know the things he knew
But not at his expense.

I bargained with my Maker
Foolish as it seems
I would always leave unlearned
Some vital little things;

And in my sheer dependency
I'd somehow earn more time
Making God feel guilty
Taking home this friend of mine.

We doctored calves and branded
Mended fence, went to sales
Pushed cattle up the mountain
Scouted all the unused trails.

He never gave me reason
To slack my quest to learn
Encouragement was steady
Yet that dream within me burned.

His eyes would beam at each new thing
That I had learned to do
The thrill I felt was soon to melt
Those fears I had gone through.

In time my chains were broken
By his love and faith in me
    A child had been in bondage
    A woman was set free.

Perfect Wife
by Peggy Godfrey

George and I been thinkin'
'Bout tryin' to find a wife
A sweet and gentle martyr
Who'd like the ranchin' life.

Ya know, someone to stay at home
To mop the floors and dust
Tidy up around the house
And never show disgust.

Not the horse-back ridin' sort
But one who'd stay indoors
Whose interests won't emerge until
She's done with all the chores.

We'd have fresh coffee in the pot
She'd bake us cookies and pies
Wash the dishes, answer the phone
And swat the dad-burned flies.

She'd write the checks to pay the bills
And file the ranch receipts
Store away our winter clothes
Occasionally change the sheets.

She'd wash and dry and fold our clothes
Mend the ones with holes
Disagree—POLITELY
Then comply with all our goals.

Supposin' she gets uppity
We'll holler, pout, and whine.
Guilt will work her over
Shame her back in line.

Her schedule would revolve on ours
So she can run to town—
Leave us warm lunch on the stove—
When machinery breaks down.

When we're sortin' cattle
In a typical short-handed bind
She'd know which pairs to separate
By simply reading my mind.

We'd always be stocked with groceries
Have shelves of home-canned food
She'd freeze fresh fruit in season
Be tired, but never rude.

Homemade bread and jam we'd eat
Perhaps she'd milk a cow
Make butter and lots of ice cream
I'd even teach her how.

We ought to have a garden
Homegrown veggies taste so good
If she can run a chain saw
We'd let her cut our wood.

I've chopped away her personhood
To get this "perfect wife"
It makes me sick to realize
This joke was once my life.

Audrey Hankins

I WAS RAISED AS A MIDWEST FARM girl, with horses and cattle, on the land. We moved to Arizona when I was a teenager, and I found my real niche when I married a cowboy and became a ranch wife. I cooked, rode, did chores, and raised kids, calves and cowdogs. We owned a pack outfit and dude string for five years—I wrangled and was the cook for pack trips and breakfast rides.

My poems are like dear children. Most of them are tributes to specific horses, dogs, cattle, ranches, or people. "Relapse" was the most painful one to give birth to. I really wrote it as self-therapy and never dreamed it would speak to anyone else.

Relapse
by Audrey Hankins

AA books and Coors cans—
Fresh starts, forgotten vows.
Everything of yours
Wears the "hard-use" brand
Earmarked by neglect.

Through prisms of tears
Somber shadows and fears
I watch you mount
That same old bronc
And know he'll kill you yet.

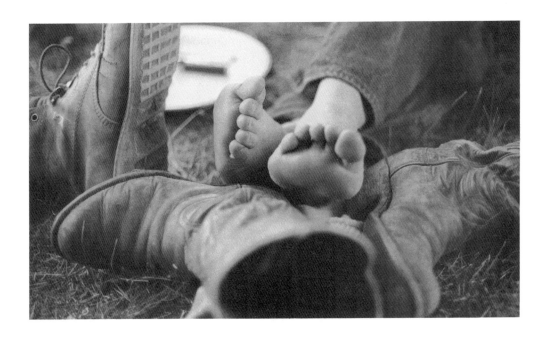

Linda Hasselstrom

Driving Into a Storm
by Linda Hasselstrom

Last night we burned feed sacks
emptied over the long cold. Falling
snow melted on our cheeks, clicked
on the sacks piled behind us.
You stood in your long blue coat,
a red bandana around the gray hat,
watched for sparks in the grass,
in the haystacks. Flaming sheets
of paper rose, swirled in the black smoke,
flew off southeast like crows.

Today my big hands grip
the steering wheel, knuckles scarred.
The plain gold ring is already scratched,
framed by two new calluses.
I'm racing down this road
into the snow. I sing, drink
coffee, think of the job,
ignore the clouds dropping low, lower.

You've given me so many gifts
and now one more: yourself
in your blue coat, flames
at your feet, standing against
the dark
rolling clouds.

I WASN'T BORN ON THE LAND; I was reborn here when I moved from a small city to this South Dakota ranch at the age of nine when my mother remarried. I was adopted by the land, and began developing a personal land ethic the first time I looked out on the empty, rolling prairie around my home.

During late 1989, *Newsweek* called five states, including South Dakota, the "outback" of the nation, and the Rand-McNally company left the state out of its new edition of road maps entirely, explaining that no one would want to come here. But those of us who live here like it; we like the country a little bit empty, so we have space for our thoughts. We're used to conserving our resources; most of us were brought up to "waste not, want not," and consider conservation no hardship. When we retire, we visit California, and take pictures of ourselves lying on the beach in Florida, but we come home, and when we speak of those places, there is a trace of pity in our voices. Too many people make us nervous and testy, and cause us to snarl at traffic jams and clean our rifles.

Seasons in South Dakota

by Linda Hasselstrom
for Rodney, who asked

I

Dirty snow left in the gullies, pale
green spread overnight on the hills
mark spring.
                      Taking corn to the hens
I hear a waterfall of redwing blackbird song.
When I open the windows to their raucous mating
I let in something else as well:
soon I'll pace the hills under the moon.

II

Watching struggling heifers birth,
greasing the tractor, I may miss
summer.
                  Like spring, it bursts open:
blooming hay demands the mower.
All day I ride the tractor,
isolated by roar.
It's time to turn the bulls out
to the cows, check leaning fences.
Even in summer nights' sweat
I hate to sleep alone.
When I'm too tired to care,
I still hear the larks, feel
the cold flow in each window at dawn.

III

Autumn whistles in some day when I'm
riding the gray gelding
bringing in fat calves for sale:
the air quick-chills, grass turns brown.
Last fall I found two gray hairs;
just as quick, winter came:

I was hurrying to pile fresh wood
from the one-woman crosscut saw
when the first flakes crowded the sky.

IV

Despite the feeding, pitching hay to
black cows with frost-rimmed eyes,
cutting ice on the dam under the eyes
of sky and one antelope,
there's still time to sit before the fire,
curse the dead cold outside,
the other empty chair.

Rancher Roulette

by Linda Hasselstrom

It's no trick to get killed ranching.
You might get a foot caught
in a stirrup when your horse bucks, get dragged
to death; that's what happened to my half brother.
He was riding that ridge to the south there;
his wife found him, after the storm.

Or tip the tractor over on a slope. Or forget
to turn off the power takeoff, and get your pants leg caught.
That happened to a neighbor, back in the forties.
By the time his kids saw the tractor circling,
he wasn't any bigger than a baseball.
Just wound him right around it.

Or you could get bit by a rattler, fixing fence.
I killed one with my shoe once, clean forgot
that left my foot sort of vulnerable.
Knew a fella ended up in a dam, drowned;
folks said he must have fell off his horse
and hit his head, but he was courting the daughter of a man
who didn't like him much.

A horse can kick you in the head,
you can get hit by a bull or stomped
by a cow that just calved. I got thrown from my horse
one time—well, more than that—but this one time
I was knocked out, and when I woke up
my head was between two rocks.
If I'd hit either one,
my head would have popped like a watermelon.

Knew a guy fell off the windmill once—
he was fixing it and the wind come up. Jammed his hips
up somewhere around his ears. I damn near drowned
trying to get a rope under a cow stuck in a mudhole.
She thrashed around and pushed me under.
I finally lassoed her head and drug her out that way.
She died anyway, broke her back.

Freezing to death would be easy. After I fell
in the creek chopping ice I damn near died
before I could get fifty feet to the pickup.
It makes a person wonder if there ain't some other way
to make a living. I heard the other day lightning
struck a fella's place on his fifty-fourth birthday,
killed fifty-four cows standing under a tree.

He said, "I hope I don't live to be a hundred;
I can't afford it."

Planting Peas
by Linda Hasselstrom

It's not spring yet, but I can't
wait anymore. I get the hoe,
pull back the snow from the old
furrows, expose the rich dark earth.
I bare my hand and dole out shriveled peas,
one by one.

                I see my grandmother's hand,
doing just this, dropping peas
into gray gumbo that clings like clay.
This moist earth is rich and dark
as chocolate cake.

                Her hands cradle
baby chicks; she finds kittens in the loft
and hands them down to me, safe beside
the ladder leading up to darkness.

                I miss
her smile, her blue eyes, her biscuits and gravy,
but mostly her hands.

                I push a pea into the earth,
feel her hands pushing me back. She'll come in May,
she says, in long straight rows,
dancing in light green dresses.

Beef Eater
by Linda Hasselstrom

I have been eating beef hearts
all my life.
I split the smooth maroon shape
lengthwise,
open it like a diagram, chambers exposed.
I cut tough white membranes off valves,
slice onions over the heart,
float it in water,
boil it tender.
I chop prunes, apricots, mushrooms
to mix with dry bread, sage from the hillside.
I pack the crevices full,
nail the heart together,
weave string around the nails.

Gently,
I lift the full heart
between my hands,
place it in the pan
with its own blood, fat, juices.
I roast that heart
at three hundred fifty degrees
for an hour or two.
Often I dip pan juices,
pour them lovingly over the meat.

When I open the oven,
the heart throbs
in its own golden fat.

I thicken the gravy with flour,
place the heart with love
on my Grandmother's ironstone platter,
slice it evenly from the small end;
pour gravy over it all,
smile as I carry it to the table.

My friends have begun to notice my placid air,
which they mistake for serenity.
Yesterday a man remarked
  on my large brown eyes,
my long eyelashes,
my easy walk.

I switched my tail at him
as if he were a fly,
paced
deliberately
away.

Joan Hoffman

New Ranch Wife
by Joan Hoffman

A bride
walks love-first
into a stranger's house
picks up his dirty socks,
washes his stained underwear
and screws the top of the toothpaste
firmly in place.

In the evening she listens to unfamiliar talk
concerning post-hole diggers,
pump-leathers, and rake teeth.

She misses the fun of
waiting to go to the movies,
driving around on back roads,
parking on the way home.

She would like to exchange confidences
with her girlfriends,
defy her father's curfew
and skip out before the dishes were done.

She thinks of the days when she used
her mother's perfume and charge cards,
and walks quickly past the Dress Shoppe
when she is in town for supplies.

She wonders why it was so exciting
to look forward to the mystery of being
married
and why the reality is so ordinary.

Sometimes she wants more than anything
to be at home in her own bed,
but she squares her shoulders
burns the toast again,
and settles in.

I GREW UP SURROUNDED WITH poverty and guilt. I almost never heard about language or ideas except, of course, in books, but no one taught me things I needed to know. No one knew to teach me. I wrote little rhymes about the Lady of the Moon and dreams made of gossamer, and was considered something of an anomaly, an oddling.

I've been a ranch wife since the early forties, and I have experienced amazing things: I know about pain and heartbreak, about rejection and alienation, about such joy I cannot tell you the wonder of it; triumph and victory have been random companions along with a demon depression I fear like a haunting. I have one husband, two children, six grandchildren, some kindly relatives, and some good friends. I have never quite determined how I feel about the land. It is a fearsome tyrant, I know that, and has forever taken more than it has returned. I don't think about it the way my husband thinks about it and I don't think I think about it the way my own two kids think about it. Out of all this, my poems have come.

The Lonely, Empty, Prairie Sky
by Joan Hoffman

In the midst of everywhere I know this place
as I know my own voice calling echoes up and down
the valley, as I know my eyes looking into a close-held
mirror, as my tongue knows the inside of my mouth.

I know the wind as intimately as I know love,
its mark and signature upon the fragile land,
and I know the smell of rain riding down the gale
across the hills, across the meadows, across the river.

When seeping cold makes my bones
brittle inside my skin,
when relentless summer beats
my face with a golden hammer,
I am at home beneath the lonely, empty, prairie sky.

Helen

by Joan Hoffman

I think now of Helen, the bride,
and of Helen, dead these twenty odd years
what I know of spouse abuse,
of going forth
to multiply and fill the earth.

When Will Hirsch brought her to our little country church
I wondered to myself what such a pretty thing
such as she was then
could have found appealing in that
awkward, coarse, ill-spoken young man.
What it finally amounted to, I think,
was that she accepted as given
all those things I railed against:
the work ethic, the rhythm method,
the husband as head of the house,
a woman's place
and The Church.

After she and I became friends
she'd call me on a snowy afternoon
and tell me how she hated winter,
how she'd tried to lose a few pounds
and how much she wanted a new washing machine.
Once, she said, she had crossed her fingers that
the new Papal Encyclical
would relax the Church's traditional
view of birth control. (I wouldn't have said it
quite that way!)

It seemed fitting somehow that
she would die in the parking lot after Mass.
It took six big men to put her into the rescue unit.

Will was devastated.
He kept going around saying he'd hoped the house they were
building would have pleased her.
As it turned out I think she was happy any way,
just to get some rest.

I Remember Being Beautiful
by Joan Hoffman

My lovely, lineless face
was my birth right.
I painted a large red heart
on each cheekbone,
blackened my lashes

with soot and spit,
and circled my head
with pale carnations.

I rubbed oil of sandalwood
between my breasts and shoulder blades
and had a blue unicorn tattooed
inside my left thigh.
I learned to speak Portuguese
at night school,
and I developed a passion for
chocolate and poetry.

One morning in front of the
downtown post office
an old, old man
pressed his mouth against my ear and said,
"Hello, good lookin'."

Remembering Willie Mae

by Joan Hoffman

*(Funeral services for Wilma Mae Kettridge were held at
Hauser's mortuary on Friday, December 3rd. Mrs. Kettridge
owned and operated King's Hotel. She had no survivors.)*

I remember like last night, Willie Mae coming to town:
She was a big woman, breasts like sun-ripe mush-melons,
round hind-end looked like bread dough rising
and a waist no bigger than my wrist.
Shit . . . she was a looker, hair hanging down in that
buttered-yellow braid
blue eyes clearer than a piece of sky,
and that laugh, My God, you could hear it over in Sac County,
sounded like a sweet trumpet blowing in the southeast wind.

No one ever heard of Kettridge, that fellow she married.
Came in a stranger like she did, and then broke his neck
falling off a ladder.
They'd only been together six months.

Willie Mae wore a black dress, held her head way down
and talked to nobody for more than a year,
and then one night
right there in the hotel saloon
she bust loose, got drunk and cried and yelled and beat on
the table.
Some one had to carry her upstairs.

But she warn't no whore,
no way was she a whore.
She was real strict with herself,
only portioned out her love like she couldn't wait.
First time I seen her hungry I ached for a week.

One night when the saloon was full of men off the circuit,
she and me slipped out. For a long time Willie Mae was my
girl.
Having her was like riding a dream,
mostly it was the way she smelled: a mix of whiskey and
drugstore soap,
clean and creamy and cool tasting,
her skin was smoother than a blowed-up balloon.

All of the time she was fighting me and moaning
and giving in and laughing and laying back,
and then at last she'd get a little crazy
and say things I didn't think she'd know.
It was better'n waking up to thunder.

And time slipped away like a twenty dollar bill.
One day I was young and proud and kinda wild,
and the next thing I was gimpy from riding too many
horses.

Willie Mae was the only one who stayed young.
And she had done real good:
made some money at the hotel, bought land and cattle
and hired a young fellow out of Sidney to run her spread.

Well . . . I'd talk to myself, and I held on to my memories.
And I always acted like it made me no difference we'd
drifted apart.
One night . . . bellied up to the old bar,
I heard her laugh, and there she was
saying, "Hello, Tubby Johnson, remember me?"

I whirled around and looked in her face and I said,
"My God, Willie Mae, My God."

We danced close like in the old days, and the thing
was she smelled better than ever
something she had on was like sweet spice,
it filled me up like a garden.

Later she asked me why we never got married.
I mulled that over and figured I'd been a damfool.
But I told her . . .
"You know, Willie Mae, some things just ain't meant to be."

Linda Hogan

MY FAMILY, LIKE MOST CHICKA-saws, had horses and cattle, but lost them all during the depression. That time was another tragic event following a hundred years of loss and removal. What happened in Oklahoma was planned poverty, with the banks loaning Indian people money for food, seed, and survival, when the bankers knew they could foreclose on the Indian farmers and ranchers who did not have the slightest chance of paying back the loans. This was ten years before I was born, but the loss and pain of that time were so great that stories of the Depression became embedded deep inside me. Those times told us once again that we were still Indian and that the land belonged to Others; that we could be moved always from territory to territory.

For American Indian people the journey home is what tells us our human history, the mystery of our lives here, and leads us toward fullness and strength. These poems were part of that return for me, an identification with my tribe and the Oklahoma earth, a deep knowing and telling how I was formed of these two powers called ancestors and clay. They are home speaking through me.

The Other Voices
by Linda Hogan

There are things we do not tell
when we tell about weather
and being fine.
Our other voices take sanctuary
while police with their shepherds
stand guard
at the borders of breath
lest our stories escape
this holy building
of ourselves.

How did we come to be
so unlike the chickens clucking their hearts out
openly in the rain,
the horses just being horses
on the hillside,
and coyotes howling
their real life at the moon?

We don't tell our inner truth
and no one believes it anyway.
No wonder I am lying
in the sagging bed,
this body with the bad ankle
and fifteen scars showing,
and in the heart, my god,
the horrors of living.
And in my veins, dear mother,
the beauties of my joyous life,
the ribs and skull and being,
the eyes with real smiles
despite the sockets they lie in
that know where they are going.

Outside, the other voices are speaking.
Pine needles sing with rain
and a night crawler
with its five hearts
beats it
across the road.

In silence
the other voices speak
and they are mine
and they are not mine
and I hear them
and I don't,
and even police can't stop earth telling.

Left Hand Canyon

by Linda Hogan

> *"Remember what Chief Left Hand said?*
> *Never mind. Everything else*
> *was taken from him,*
> *let's leave his grief alone."*
> —William Matthews

In the air
which moves the grass
moves the fur of a black horse
his words come back,
the old griefs
carried on the wind.

Left Hand returns to speak,
wind in the blood of those
who will listen.
If his words were taken from him,
I'm giving them back.
These words,
if you listen
they are real.
These words,
a hand has written them.

Everything speaks.
Put your ear to the earth
and hear it, the trees speaking,
mining for minerals.

You can't take a man's words.
They are his even as the land
is taken away
where another man
builds his house.

And the night animals,
their yellow eyes
give back the words
while you are sleeping
when all the old animals
come back
from their secret houses
of air.

Celebration: Birth of a Colt
by Linda Hogan

When we reach the field
she is still eating
the heads of yellow flowers
and pollen has turned her whiskers
gold. Lady,
her stomach bulges out,
the ribs have grown wide.
We wait,
our bare feet dangling
in the horse trough,
warm water
where goldfish brush
our smooth ankles.
We wait
while the liquid breaks
down Lady's dark legs
and that slick wet colt
like a black tadpole
darts out
beginning at once
to sprout legs.
She licks it to its feet,
the membrane still there,
red, transparent
the sun coming up shines through,
the sky turns bright with morning
and the land
with pollen blowing off the corn,
land that will always own us,
everywhere it is red.

Linda Hussa

Somehow my life began when I married and moved to this sagebrush corner of California, and found this work, ranch work. John taught me, even pushed me, to find bravery, ability, and endurance I didn't know were mine. We were horseback every day. We cut out cancer eyes. We performed cesarean sections. We rode colts and roped calves. And, of course, there was other work too. All the stuff that every other woman on a ranch does. I brought writing with me but it stayed packed away for a long time. But writing is not to be ignored. It hangs back in the shadows and bides its time. Now, while I still do all the outside work, I no longer darn socks. I nuke the food. I never iron.

In my twenty-one years here, I have found a teacup under a board, a silver pitcher split by frost, a baking powder can filled with colored buttons, a gnawed cookbook in a packrat's nest. All of these things bear the hand of a woman. Their unpampered lives stain this land. Their stories were left behind and I hear them and I tell them to you.

Homestead in Hell Creek Canyon
by Linda Hussa

Quiet
Plenty to do
    but

I write Ma again
    —letter pressed with others in the lard can
    hidden—

Washing's hung out
    dry
    'fore it's pinned
    wood stacked neat by the stove
    bread loaves steam sweet
    browned just like
    Mister
    likes 'em

Floor's sprinkled down
    washed my feet
    hair's braided
    up, forget-me-nots tucked in
    rubbed my hands with sheeps' grease
    that tramp herder gave me
    Mister hates the smell, but they're awful cracked

Brought the cow up from the willows
    she's slow walkin'
    but I don't mind
    in the leanto shade
    my cheek on her flank, I squeeze those big finger tits
    the warmth of her, the smell
    her stomach workin'

I hear Mister comin'
    pull foolish flowers from my braids
    hold them behind my skirts
    until he's gone by
    he nods
    I nod back
    milk spills
    white drops slide between my toes

The cow leaves the shed
    split hoof
    tiny blue petals
    in the same track

Under the Hunter Moon

by Linda Hussa

I slip the rifle sling over my shoulder
    and step into the silence of dawn
Geese move through the darkened sky
    toward the pond
      Wings cut the quiet
      with an oddly mechanical sound
      and then their voices set me right

I open the gate
The sheep rise from their beds
    as if I commanded it so
Lambs rush to thump flanks for milk
    kept warm through the autumn night

I fall in with their march up the meadow
    to find clover that grew while they slept
Stalks of blue chicory and tiny golden trefoil
    fold inside pink lips, and chewing,
    they walk on

At the fence line I know the place
    where the soft pads left prints in the dust
    by a hole in the woven wire
    and I am a warrior hunched in rose briars
    their scent pale, and their thorns pick at my wool coat

Stern in my resolve
    I wait while the sun creeps to the edge of the day
Slain lambs, guts ripped open
Magpies and blow flies
Blatting ewes with swollen bags searching the flock

A lamb a day for two weeks
    I grip the rifle tighter

A shadow comes toward me through the moonlight
    grey and tan, she arches in a mouse pounce
    and works her way toward the barrel of my rifle,
    toward the bullet I will hurl
    at her heart

I watch her snatch mice out of the grass
    flip them up like popcorn,
    down the hatch. She is a comic
    this coyote, playing, laughing
    making her way steadily toward me
    my finger soft on the cold steel trigger

Coyote stops
    looks directly at me
Her eyes hold me accountable

Homesteaders, Poor and Dry

by Linda Hussa

The world was bone dry.
I don't know why God would do such a thing.
The field was bare as the floor
And the springs nothin'—nothin'.

Papa's cattle bawled night and day
        'til I thought I'd go crazy with it.
        Turn them out, I cried.
        Kill them, Papa, I begged.
        And he did.
        And he killed himself, too
        in a way
        'cause he loved them crazy ol' cows.
I had to help him.
There wasn't anybody else.
        Momma had the baby.

He handed me the big knife
        and I followed him.
First he took the red one,
        the one he didn't like the most.
        Old Mule, he called her 'cause she kicked him every day.
He coaxed her into the barn.
She went hoping for some hay.
The barn still smelled like hay,
        so she went.
He tied her up
        and took the knife from me
        held it 'round behind his back
        He thought she'd know what he was up to,
        and run.
He slipped his arm around her neck
        and the knife came up
        sharp and glinting
        like a present.

His hands were shaking.
He had killed cows and pigs and chickens
     millions of 'em
     but his hands were shaking now.
This dry had him half crazy too.
Just when I thought he wouldn't do it
     he screamed
     and I screamed
     and old Mule screamed.

     She pulled back
     and her wild eyes looked right at me.
     Blood thumped out of her and she fell
     shaking the ground under me
     as if I was going, too.

Papa was on his knees crying,
     I'm sorry, old Mule, I'm sorry,
     and I ran away.
I threw the gate open
     and chased the other cows away.
     I didn't know where they'd go,
     but somebody else could kill 'em.
     Not my Papa.

The next week the well went dry.
Papa would drop the bucket down
     and it would come up empty.
He turned the bucket over and the bottom was wet.
He said I'd have to go down in the well
     and fill the bucket
     with a cup.
     I'd have to
     'cause we could never pull him up.

He was the strongest
and the well was small
and I was the smallest.
No Papa. I can't.
Yes, you can, girl. You can do it for the Baby.
He tied a stick in the rope
for me to stand on
and boosted me over the side.
I could only see a few feet down
then there was a black hole
and I was looking into the belly of a monster.
A monster that would take me in one swallow
and I didn't even get to have my own baby and home yet.
His face brushed mine
and I whispered, No Papa.
No.
But the rope was sliding down over the edge
and I was going down too.
I clung on to that rope
nothing could get me loose.

There were things down there.
Scarey things that would touch me.
Papa's face in the circle of sky went farther away
until I couldn't see him
only a black circle in a blue circle
getting smaller.
The well was so narrow
the walls brushed me.

It was dark
and places big rocks stuck out and scraped me.
I cried let me up
let me up
but I was still going down,
leaving the world
leaving Mama crying my name
and my Papa moaning, it's for the baby, girl.

I was lowered down in that well every day
    'til the drought broke.
    Every day.
    I closed my eyes and sang myself songs
    dipped the water raising down there in the pitch dark
    all by the feel.
But there was no time I'll remember
    like that first time.
After, when the water came back up in the well
    I went and looked down into the water
    and imagined myself on the bottom
    and sometimes I wanted to go back down
    to the quiet of the dark.

In all my life
    Nothing can make me scared.
    I went down into the earth
    and drew back up.
    Nothing can ever scare me again.
    No man.
    No beast.
    No God.
I saw His face that day
    and He promised me
    no fear.

The Widow Olson
by Linda Hussa

So we passed this neat little ranch
        on the edge of Catlow Valley.
A perfect community of out buildings
        held apart by government issue poplars and cottonwoods.

"Whose place is that?"
        I asked the old buckaroo beside me.

He thought back to a winter ride
        when a teenage wrangle boy drove a herd of horses
        one hundred blue miles
        measuring each day by the homestead trees in the distance.

"The Widow Olson lives there.
        At least she used to.
        Her husband died
        and she ran the place after that."

His eyes of half Chinese,
        half Paiute,
        inscrutable to the second power
        looked into mine.

I imagined a single woman
        120 miles from town,
        a day's ride from the nearest neighbor,
        riding, working, living
        alone
        alone
        alone.

"How long did she run the place
        alone."
        alone
        alone

"Oh," he thought back to her kitchen
        and the food on his plate,
        and the stove by his bed glowing red
        and her soaking up the silence of the boy.
        "30 or 40 years."

"A woman ran a ranch out here
        for 30 or 40 years
        ALONE
        and you still call her
        the WIDOW Olson?

        What was her first name, Jimmy?"

He thought along for two jackrabbits,
        and a half dozen chuckholes.
        "I d'know. We just called her the Widow Olson."

Then he told me about the next ranch
        a day's ride ahead.

The Blue Filly
by Linda Hussa

She is just three.
Weaned again.

First time from her dead mother
    small blue head
    in the flank of a still heart.

Second time from a spotted burro
    who let her stand near
    as they swept flies in their head-tail sleep.

Last from the mare band
    that taught her with stinging nips
    to stand back and wait.

She sees him coming.
    Hay poking out in mid-chew
    does she wonder, "What now?"

He speaks her name
    in sound and breath
    she will come to know as her own.

A halter slips over her nose
    and she follows him into the barn
    shivering.

Hobbles hold her
    while the brush sweeps
    firm and soft over her skin.

And when his hand slides down her neck
    I feel it on mine.
    We both relax
    and prepare ourselves for the saddling.

Margot Liberty

MY RANCH EXPERIENCE BEGAN when my mother, Helena Huntington Smith—who wrote *We Pointed Them North* (with Teddy Blue Abbott) and *A Bride Goes West* (with Nannie Tiffany Alderson) —began taking my brother and me to Wyoming dude ranches when I was six. Later, we rented a ranch house from which I rode horseback to a one-room school. We went back east because of the war. I took ag and animal husbandry at Cornell, and after I graduated, I taught a one-room school south of Miles City, Montana, and then at the Northern Cheyenne day school at Birney, Montana. I married a cowboy, Forrest Liberty. We, of course, were hoping to buy a ranch and ran our ill-fated starter herd on rented pasture. Seven years and two kids later it became clear that this was not going to work out. I went back to graduate school in anthropology with the kids (Ellen Cotton, a rancher I had worked for, moved us to Minneapolis in the stock truck) and got a PhD in cultural anthropology. I moved back to Sheridan, Wyoming, thirteen years ago and now my work with ranching is as an anthropologist, writer, and filmmaker.

Evening, Four Mile
by Margot Liberty

Incredible, the softness of this air
That rings these valleys with the breath of May;
And still the shapes of darkness and despair,
Beyond the sweetly pyramiding hay;

The hills as green as Ireland, and the skies
As soft and blue as any that survive
In any paradise: and mating cries
Of horses musical: and they arrive,

The Porlock persons, torturing our thirst
For love, and beauty, and the moment's spark;
And on we go, in loss of soul accursed,
Through all the lovely evening and the dark.

* Porlock persons—reference to the businessman from Porlock who distracted Coleridge at the moment his vision which later emerged as the poem "Kubla Khan" seemed most vivid to him.

Rain Prayer

by Margot Liberty

For so long, we've longed for rain,
Cool upon the fevered brain,
Cool upon the aching heart,
Which has all but ripped apart,
Shrieking to the sky above
All the mocking lies of love—
Let these awful moments cease,
In Thine hour of raining peace.

Let the blessings of Thy sky,
Give us rest before we die;
Give us quietness and sleep,
Ere we must Thy mission keep;
Having longed with every breath,
For the healing hand of death—
Grant us from the gray Above,
Rain remembrance of Thy love.

Epitaph
by Margot Liberty

She never shook the stars from their appointed courses,

But she loved good men,

And she rode good horses.

Jo-Ann Mapson

Graining the Mare
by Jo-Ann Mapson

Out back of Lillie's barn, the sparse
snow chills our ankles. Inside
the arena we built last
summer, the mare
skitters over ice, wild with her
first taste of spring, ignorant
of the bloody membranes soaking
down her haunches into slush. She has
slipped another foal.

It was less than a thrill
watching the stud do his work:
chains, hobbles, both horses panic-eyed,
handlers turning sheepish, her tail
stiffly arced in defiance.

March sky: empty, gray,
barren as this horse.
Whatever do we expect, falling
for mustaches like shades of lipstick?
"Honest, he's different, this time for sure,"
the chorus we sing in any weather.

Hot grain and bran:
equine Ovaltine.

We trek homeward to the warmth
of a woodstove, where the radio spreads
like Chapstick over the sore places,
soak our fallow hearts in beer,
two empty women warming their hands
on the skins of baked potatoes.

MY MOM'S SIDE CAME TO CALIfornia from New England tobacco farming. My grandmother rode mules and had a love affair with her dad's draft horses. She never finished school, but she ran the bookkeeping end of the farm. My female relatives' voices crop up often in the poems I write—tough immigrant women whose education came from the land and the heart. I know my horse love originates with them: the animal connectedness, the reciprocal love—just woman and horse, no men or sex to mess up a good thing. My connection to horses, ranches and the land in the present day—through training horses, teaching riding, team roping, and working to someday own a ranch in New Mexico—is the culmination of a lifetime of longing, I think, to belong to the elemental, basic, primal, simpler time.

Spooking the Horses

by Jo-Ann Mapson

It wasn't enough to scale the grapestake—we dared
crossing the orchard where any moment the farmer
might spot us. His one-eyed spaniel, tied to a stake,
lost his mind when we teased him.

All this for a sour apple eaten on a dead run
that might net us a backside of birdshot.
For quick escape, we cut
through the pasture. Smelling the apples
in our hands, the horses came investigating.

Sun polished their muscles. Sour, foreign,
sweetly compelling, their scent riddled us
into naming the pungency. Seaweed? Last Christmas's
mulling spices, furry mold? Uncle Louie's girl:
Grandma called her Floozie.

We lured them close
enough to sneak a pat of steamy skin.
Just when the lead mare
trusted us, we whooped and waved our arms high—
of course, they ran—but came back so often
I'd swear shame fueled the trot.
Swan necks bent low,
grudging through desire. *We don't need
those kinds of apples, oh, but we want them.*

In bed that night, my cousin drowsily traced
profiles on my back, summoning shivers
beneath the sunburn. Guess which horse,
she whispered, guess. "Hush!" Grandma sang
up to the attic, "the both of you. Now!"
We'd giggle, mimic her fraying voice

in the summer dark lit by a moon yellow as cheddar,
two skinny girls whispering: Bay mare! Dapple-gray!
The magical ring of Palomino. Our horses
leapt from wall shadows
until their hooves were dreamborne,
that moment of suspension when they belonged
not to air, nor earth, but to us.

By August our shadows were stretching,
bagging at the knees, cut tight
across the chest. It hurt,
that awkward stepping into adolescent skin,
no longer satisfied with stealing
someone else's fruit, tortured into our own.

Tell Us Again

by Jo-Ann Mapson

"Back then," Gemma said, "they gave you ether,
none of this panting like a run-over dog
begging for shotgun. No sucking
ice from a paper cup. One good snoot, you
rose like meringue, straight to fairyland.
Your womb was the doctor's domain,
that drunken Judas counting his silver
as far from the room as humanly
able. Your daddy, Chase—honey, the name
alone—over in Yuma unloading cattle,
beasts too old to damage much
desert. For some reason your mama
went belly up, her color old fireplace
ashes. Maybe some nurse chafed over the missing
gold band, went out for coffee, just plain forgot.
Your births like to rip her apart, fool doctor
not expecting so much blood, two babies
where there shouldn't have been one."

Mama from pictures: the tilt of her
chin desperate behind the ivory skin
saying "Take one, take either of them,
just give me the gas."

I imagine her eighteen, remote,
tethered to the delivery table, her scared
animal smell, biting her tongue
to keep from wailing. Did she
notice us, rafting her blood like rapids,
memorize in that instant our generous
hands, wise mouths inheriting her tongue
for trouble? I want her to have waved,
just one small flutter to the unexpected fish
spurting from her flesh into a man's hands.
I hear her bones under our cheeks,
callow angel, promising us good
men, gentle lovers, a life
gleaming with sequins.

Mela D. Mlekush

I SPENT MY CHILDHOOD RUNNING outdoors, horseback and on foot, trapping gophers for a nickel, slopping hogs, being in 4-H, working with livestock, fishing in Ten Mile Creek and ice skating in the winter. I love the land and the simplicity of life cycles, and I'm glad to be raising my own children on a ranch. I write more in summer because I am outside a lot, camping and what not, and outside is where I write best (no mother and wife jobs yelling at me). My poems come from sorting past experiences, recording today's history, and sometimes putting dreams down in black and white to keep them in perspective. I write of childhood with horses and I also write about the horrors. Some of the horrors upset people, who look at green pastures and sage and see cowboys and ranchers, never believing in the suicide, sexual abuse and insanity that exist alongside everything else.

The Rummage Sale
by Mela D. Mlekush

Orange plaid polyester pantsuit
hangs sunset bright
in the decaying Fellowship Hall.
Soaked ceiling tile sags
still damp from fall rain,
chipped linoleum curls
up to catch careless toes and heels.
Charter members of the Methodist
Women's Society rock slowly
amid tables of recycled clothing.
Hug memories like bags
of groceries carried
too many blocks.
Grey heads bend,
eyes study the floor,
in a game of Button-Button.

Jane sews a button on a ruffled dress.
    Julia died at seven
    she wasn't ever right.
    Ma worked so hard.
    Never had time for me.

Bites the thread.
Hands the dress on.

Lucille buttons it to a hanger.
    My Johnny left me
    three boys in short pants
    to raise by myself.
She folds a pair
of tattered size 4 jeans
pats them smooth.
    Then Momma passed on, too.
    These should be fifty cents.

    This is a rag.
    Knew she was goin' Thanksgivin'.
    Said good-bye I won't
    see you again.

Two months later . . .
These sheets have holes.
Fifty-eight years after the funeral she cries.
    Momma.
Cuts the buttons off a well-worn cotton gown.

Sarah takes the buttons
rolls them in her hand.
    My Jimmy.
    The other kids had no scratches
    My Jimmy's car.
    His daddy was
    never the same.
    Hurt him so.
She sees the whole family
wearing look-alike
red, white and blue western shirts,
the picture on the piano at home.

Martha picks up a rusted Tonka tractor
marked a nickel,
chooses instead a one-armed teddy bear
with button eyes to tell
of little Lillie lost to flu.
    Folks were dying all around
    Lillie was just walkin'
    she got sick
    burnt up
    pukin'
    nothin' would stay down her.
    Poor thing.
She pulls the bear to her bosom.

Elsie fingers a chipped China saucer
    Flo collected these
    lost all her hair
    lingered
    suffered.
    Leukemia sipped away her life
    like too hot tea.
A crystal drop splashes
on the cup from Lenox Limited.

A tiny pearl button pops to the floor
as Bernice tries on a pink brocade formal.
    Sylvie lost her baby.
    It was due.
    They took pictures.
    She looked like she was sleepin'.
    Perfect.
    Cute as a button.
    I don't know why she died.

Holey underdrawers for the rag bag.
Buttons stripped from threadbare blouses
rattle in a two-pound Folger's can.

Gentleman of the Prairie
by Mela D. Mlekush

He is mulch about rosebushes,
frost-coated and still.
Work shirt faded and frayed,
blue Levis washed to fog,
Ausimark* stain on the knee
from ten years ago,
when he last visited the lambing shed.
Sitting in his easy chair
the hardest thing he has to do.
He reads L'Amour and remembers
when he drove the cattle,
worked the horses, riding and draft.
At ten he rode a boxcar
from Dakota to Grass Range,
still fifty miles to the homestead claim
where he grew to be a man.

Wheezing like a wind-broke horse
he waits for me. Rocks slowly
in his green crushed velvet chair,
armrests worn to bare weave.
I have come to help exercise lungs
shrunk like dried apples
in an old root cellar.

Fifty years my senior he courts me
with stories of snowdrifts, horses,
country dances and country dames.
We buckle on blinders, collars and hames
traverse his yesterdays when his skin
was like leather instead of parchment.
When he rode young horses
When dreams hung like berries
on a juniper bough
and time turned life
like loam beneath a plow.

* Ausimark—paint for marking sheep

A Wild One Goes
by Jennifer Olds

A spavined mare limps out
one last time, her sway-back
gone white from flea-bitten gray,
from the rosy roan color
she met the world in. Hers
was the first horse leg I
bunted a toddler head to,
the first chestnut my baby hands
peeled and saved so that,
if by chance I met a wild
one, I could tame it by
this scent on my palms.
That is how it is done: The
wild horse will stand to strange
music and snake its head
towards an odd familiar smell,
and when its muzzle drops
you must gentle loop the rope
around its great hairy neck
and it will be yours.

This big barren mare,
gone chesty as a bar-maid,
shuffles on foundered feet.
And though her fur still lays shiny
groomed, though her tail whisks
and flags this small winter wind,
though her eyes brown round
smartly, her feet are done
for and the suffering has
begun. The vet fills his
syringe precisely and
we don't turn away at the
needle tap tap on the jugular,
and we don't turn away
as his thumb dumps the contents in,
and we don't turn away
when the wild one sways
and it is raining, it is raining
though, Christ, the skies are clear.

I REMEMBER TRAVELING WITH MY mother to horse ranches in the dead of night. She was a mare midwife, and she had an uncanny knack of knowing just when a mare was ready to drop. When I was three, her own great mare, Khareyn, lost a foal. That was the first time I saw my mother cry and the first time I saw, at close hand, the intensity of an animal's grief. For weeks, this mare was wild with it, to the point of trying to steal other mare's foals. The following year, she guarded her new colt ferociously, putting her huge body between him and all other equines. She never forgot, never.

My finest horse was a half-blind, half-crazy, black-and-white pinto named The Infidel. I was a tempestuous child, and he was a dangerous and tempestuous horse. In each other we found a measure of peace, of understanding. He was crazy as a loon, but would have died before he hurt me. We both knew that. He died within a week of his 20th birthday. Even now, nearly five years later, my heart still jumps at the sight of a black-and-white horse.

Blinding the Infidel
by Jennifer Olds

A week after you came home
we noticed how you ran into fences,
did not see a hand moving
toward your right eye.
The horse trainer said yeah,
there had been problems;
you could not seem
to learn your lessons.

He couldn't pinpoint the exact
moment it happened.
Was it just after his whip
raised welts, or when he
cowboyed one spur jab too many?

I believe that you took it
and took it, like a battered wife,
until something snapped.
And you flipped over backward
and you flipped over backward
and somewhere in that fight
you missed that son of a bitch,
crushed the side of your black head
into the fence and darkness.

Verlena Orr

Our Mother's Mother
by Verlena Orr

She had no patience
for sick kittens
—watery green stars
of their eyes
waning with fever—
twisted their yielding necks
before scattering wheat
for the hens
who laid their share of moons
before she butchered them
for harvest men. She wanted
fat gold gravy
to keep a man
bearing down on the dark
land. Many kittens
with shadowy vision
wobbled into the milk dish
lurched for feed
as their flimsy lives
were snapped like green beans
on a hot day.

Now snow flails
my one window.
Pale with cowering
I forgive
that old woman
hoeing every day,
see how useless
my daily piano scales
became for getting along,
how her garden blurred
into a sliver of dust.

MY SISTER TELLS ME THAT AS A child I spent my time playing in the mud in the creek. I also read all the time, something only lazy women do in my particular farm culture, and of course I loved my boss who figures in the poem "First Job," even though she was the object of much criticism because her house was dirty and she sat around with her nose in a book. To pay for first year college, I sold my horse and added that to the money from the one steer a year my parents had put aside for me. I left the land physically, but during the past few years my writing has often drawn on those early experiences. Lately things have taken a turn in that both my parents passed away this year, and my sister and I are suddenly stewards of the farm, the pasture in the mountains, and the timber.

First Job
by Verlena Orr

Minnie chopped off their heads
while I stood transfixed,
amazed at the energy of life
leaving. The pullets careened,
leaped, and ricocheted, blood
gushing on oyster shell they
had been eating minutes before.
We scalded and picked feathers,
burned off hair with newspaper
torches, then dressed them,
saved the yolks our fingers found.

Thirteen, I was the hired girl,
hauled wood and water, poked
kindling in the cookstove.
Fire rising, the dishwater boiled
its alkalai scum to the top.
That hard water pulled blood
to my hands. Fir splinters
rose in my fingers and sweat raced
down my beginning breasts.

The harvest men came in at noon
covered with wheat chaff and dirt.
I took the broom to their overalls,
brushed great breaths of dust
into the sun. Washing up,
the men snorted like horses,
and I looked for clean plates—
shelves peppered with mice droppings.
I longed for Modern Romance
I could read in the barn.

Even lye couldn't cut the chicken lard.
As I scrubbed the dinner dishes,
Minnie read True Confessions unmoved
by unmade beds covered with the land
her sons took to bed.

Shy, I thumbed The Red Cross Book
of Nursing, read how to sanitize
with Lysol, go through childbirth,
treat Whooping cough and Scarlet fever.
I still carry those hot afternoons—
the useless importance of mustard plaster,
how to make a bed with mitered corners
that had no hope of ever coming loose.

Prophecy

by Verlena Orr

"But what I cannot have or cannot keep
Draws me down under the waters, and I come
With him, with her, into a strange communion . . . "
—May Sarton

We're not watching The Fireworks this year
but head for the living room. You reign
from your Naugehyde recliner, frayed black
electrical tape holding years together.
My place, the platform rocker you always oil
before I come home.

From Nashville, whatever the cowboy star sings
is our song. You pat your foot in time.
Ninety, and I'm just getting to know you—father
who taught me to waltz, patient as I learned
the box-step, kept time with the drum.

Tonight we have the ease of a waltz balanced
solid on land. Outside where the cold mountain
prairie would weasel through our coats, brilliant
parachutes mock us making their way to dust.

The shirt-tail relative leaves for a better view.
Her children, rehearsed, say "I love you" on command.
Bemused you smile. You've heard it before. Last year,
our final Fourth outside, I said, "You're the best dad
in the world." "I try to be," you said, seriously
struggling from the grasp of the lawn chair.

This year I say it again, Mel Tillis in the background,
a smoke plume from your pipe, my rocker silent.
"I think so," you say, and I know then—it is settled.

A Tall Bush
by Gwen Petersen

A cowgirl has a heap of fun
A ridin' for the brand;
She rounds up cattle, ropes them calves
As good as any hand.

She wrassles dogies on the ground,
And also vaccinates;
She cuts the bulls, tattoos the ears
And keeps the tally straight.

And when the cowboys take a break
To have a pop or beer,
A cowgirl also drinks her share,
Then faces wrenching fear.

Now a cowboy does it simple style—
Just stands there by his horse,
A ponderin' life's meaning while
Nature takes its course.

But a cowgirl has three things she needs
While working way out West,
For riding chores, a darned good horse
Will help her do her best.

And second on the list, a dog
Who'll jump to her command,
And heel the strays and line 'em out,
A pup with lots of sand.

But happiness is when she finds
A tall bush thick with leaf
To shelter her and block from view
The bliss of pure relief.

Gwen Petersen

WHEN I MARRIED A RANCH- er, I began writing about country life. I find ranch- ing/farming enchanting, satisfying, and what I've always wanted to do. But as a woman, I always feel some- what alien in the cowboy world. I admire cowboys, but I don't worship them. I feel as if I'm merely tolerat- ed. We women must keep low pro- files in most of our activities and especially in the public forums. We must change the language of our poetry so it sounds "ladylike."

Country women are the most courageous beings I've ever met. I have it easy compared to most. So if I can tell their stories with humor and nostalgia, if I can reflect the truth of the country woman's grit and spirit and strength in my writing, I feel honored.

A Cussin' Woman

by Gwen Petersen

A cussin' woman's a trial to hear
For folks who want to think
That females ought to smile the while
A skunk is making stink.

But when the heifers break the fence
As I start out for town,
In pure white slacks, high heels and pearls—
My savoir faire breaks down.

When those darned hogs get in my yard
And roto-till my flowers,
You're apt to see the air turn blue
Perhaps for hours and hours.

Or when I sit at Bessie's side
Just dreaming as I yank,
And she connects with pie-stained tail:
You'll hear some words real rank.

I'm sure some gals are never rude
When farm chores go awry;
Their golden words are never crude;
Before they'd cuss, they'd die.

But let me step in fresh cow pie—
I take it as an omen;
So close your eyes and plug your ears—
Cuz I'm a cussin' woman.

Those Damned Wire Gates

by Gwen Petersen

The sun was high, the weather fair
As I roamed the hills on my buckskin mare;
The ride was long, I was running late
When I pulled up short at a barbed wire gate.

Now I know gates and I know they're mean,
But the ranch-house roof could be plainly seen;
If I went around it was five miles more,
And my seat and my knees and my back were sore.

Once I asked my spouse, "Why are gates so tight?"
He looked at me like I wasn't bright.
"Cuz a bull or a cow can lean their weight
And knock the wires off a loosened gate."

I slipped from my horse and I faced my foe—
I would at least strike an opening blow
I tried the top, then the bottom band,
I tore my sleeve and I hurt my hand.

I wrapped both arms around the post,
I pulled till I ran out of breath—almost—
I kicked its wires to show my grudge,
I cussed it soundly. It wouldn't budge!

The time was approaching six o'clock
When all of a sudden I spied a rock.
With gusto and grit I began anew
And hammered the lower wire in two.

With great relief I mounted my mare
And left that gate just lying there;
Glad to leave the scene of the crime,
We trotted home in record time.

This morning early my other half
Said, "I was out checking a newborn calf."
And then he grumbled, "Guess what I found—
The south-field gate was on the ground."

I answered then and my voice was gay,
"You know I was out there yesterday
And your black bull was quite a sight
Leaning against it with all his might."

Now I know I stretched the truth quite far,
But if everything's fair in love and war,
I'll be forgiven by all the fates
Cuz I'm at war with those damned wire gates!

Thelma Poirier

M Y LIFE IS TANGLED UP WITH the land and all the bureaucracies that do not want us to live on it. The writing may be my way of "righting" my relationship with the earth, with the best of our ranching traditions. I'm quite prepared to leave old cruelties behind, but not "old beauty."

I guess my poetry is sparse, perhaps a reflection of these Saskatchewan grasslands, a sparse land where one must find abundance within sparsity, for after all, how much is enough? Isn't it interesting the way one small piece of paper or broken glass interrupts the prairie? Maybe that is a lesson for me—less paper, less glass, less of all until I leave no marks on the land.

burrowing owl
by Thelma Poirier

how you came to die
natural causes

was it predator
you the prey?

beside the gate I find you
stiffening, intact

whatever spirit dwelled in you
must find another home

you leave a ghost without a feather
a ghost without a bone

little owl laughing
your death you call your own

old coyote hunting man

by Thelma Poirier

when Mattie gives birth to coydogs
he kills all seven
breaks their necks
the same way a coyote fells a sheep
he says
        that will teach the bitch
        running with coyotes at night

next day Mattie leaves
she runs coyotes in daylight

•

who knows what he learns in the hills
chasing coyotes

always running downwind
looking back over his shoulder
he leaves no tracks
rises
        falls with the grass
wavers
        like a coyote
disappearing in the distance

•

once every winter
old coyote hunting man
wakes the town
parks his dog box
in front of the Royal Hotel
while he tips a keg of beer

the hounds howl
snap their leashes
call the bitches from the porches

another winter old coyote hunting man
forgets to come to town
they find him in his cabin
half-eaten by the hounds

•

tawny grass takes form
rises on all fours
moves with the pack

night becomes the voice of coyotes
dawn the silence of the grass

Madame Caillier

by Thelma Poirier

driving into light
you close your eyes
the slow turn of the wagon wheel
the plod of the horses, sting of horse flies
memorized

> this is a house
> this apology of wood and clay
> this door fastened to a hole in a hill
> grass growing on the roof
> what if it rains?

> ah, maman, it does not rain

> Sainte Marie, Mere de Dieu
>   you pray

•

none of the neighbours have wives
when you are lonely you look in the mirror
to see the face of another woman

she is younger than you are
her hair is not grey
she smiles
when you touch her face

she offers you a scarlet lily
one she picked this morning
in this valley of lilies and grasses

•

your son returns from the patches
you can hear the reins coming down hard
slapping the rumps of the horses, the clang
of machinery halting

you have wasted the morning
picking lilies
he finds you looking in the mirror

he goes out, comes back
a switch in his hand
you can feel the willow on your back
bending

•

Late afternoon you let your hair fall
below your waist
you wear a black cloak
over a black dress

another face darkens the mirror
it is not yours either
the mouth, the pit of a cherry
the eyes, the eyes of the laughing adder
you carry the memory of witches
mothers burning in medieval France

•

neighbours whisper, say you are crazy
have watched you on dark nights
dancing on the benchmark

and your walking stick, they say
it is a snake
you embrace

rumours turn to venom

•

evenings find you on the hill
turning the beads in your hands
a bird in a black cloak praying
you are not alone
she is with you
white madonna of the clouds

grasslander
by Thelma Poirier

her voice, the voice of larks
the prairie singing
she offers more than grace

•

it is winter when you die
your son would throw you out
with coyotes
but he is afraid of police
he knows about the gun
the garter pistol
you carried in your purse

it is a dark grave
a warm earth
where neighbours lay you

•

climbing the hill you climbed
I discover flowers
more of your red lilies, opening

flashes of scarlet
like other immigrants I suppose
you brought your fears with you

carried them to this benchmark
spent your nights with angels
resting

following your footsteps
I ask if these are your lilies or
lilies I have planted myself

when I die
bury me on a south slope
a cemetery untended
let me lie in the June grass
with pale comandra
breadroot and nodding onion

let me settle into my bones
slumber until the ghosts call me
south

at the branding
by Thelma Poirier

years ago
women were never allowed
to go to the branding

their daughters move with ease
across the corral
one of them picks up grandpa's knife
holds it firmly in one hand
in the other hand she clutches the pouch
full and soft like a chamois purse

snip slice
the bottom falls from the purse
blood like copper pennies
stains the calf's white leg

her fingers press the flesh
bring down the larger coins

the blade again

she dips the knife in antiseptic
is ready for the next calf

forty steers later
she leaves the corral
the knife folded in her pocket

sorting cattle
by Thelma Poirier

sorting cows, canners and keepers
you hate final decisions
your son shouts, move out
move out of the way

his voice stings
all the way from the corral to the house
you could let him ease into your boots
ride in your saddle
the boy in his face blurs your vision

his anger is not your sorrow
your sorrow is a boy wanting
the burdens of a man
you should have known you could not build a
corral
large enough for both of you

Lisa Quinlan

IN 1970, WHEN I WAS FIVE YEARS old, my family moved from Colorado Springs to a desolate place called San Acacio in the San Luis Valley. Neighbors were five miles apart and there weren't many neighbors. The farm was torn and neglected and cold. We dug in. My middle brother taught me how to drive when I was seven, and from there I became part of the work crew, windrowing, raking, baling, irrigating and sheep herding. I was not discriminated against for being a girl. I was treated by my father and brothers as an equal with the same amount of work load and responsibility as they. The farm and family grew together. I think of the day we drove onto that sad place and all the years of working together as a family that turned it around. It is disturbing to see generation after generation of family ranches and farms crumbling like clods of dry dirt. If I have learned anything in this lifetime it is the great importance of a family with "life" in common. With "work" not being "work." With the ongoing support of one another.

You Ask
by Lisa Quinlan
for John D.

If I was lonely
As a little girl
And
I think about the question
And the word lonely.

I'd run as fast as I could
Through waist-high hayfields
And count how many times
The thick, tangled stems
Would trip me
Before I got tired.
The sweet, green smell
Was worth the fall
Every time.

I would pretend
To be the old woman
Who lived in the shoe
Only my children
Were 19 orphan lambs
And I would scold them
With made-up names
As they fought for
Nipples around the
Feeding bucket.
I can still feel
My smile
As I watched them
Buck and play and bawl.
I can still hear
The hollow "clomp, clomp"
As soft hooves pounded
A wood floor covered
With golden, warm straw,

The heat lamp
Cast a strange yellowish
Light in the tiny, square room.
Storytime came when they got sleepy
From milk and play
Would curl up in a lamb pile
Close to my feet
And fall asleep to
My little girl dreams.
Then I would say
A quiet good night
With each name,

I thought

I would never forget.
But have.

Was I lonely
You ask?

The hayloft
Made a perfect
Playhouse.
I had an old broom
And no matter how often
I would sweep
It was always as dusty
As the first time.
I had a little tin stove,
Cardboard refrigerator
And sink and treasures
Of dirty old jars
I found in the dump.
I had plates and saucers
And cups, plastic silverware
And miniature skillets.

I had crowds of company
In my dusty house
Company no one else
Could see or hear.
They praised
My mud cakes and cookies
And invisible tea.

I think about lonely
As I sit here
Older and different
Watching snowflakes
Fall gently
From the huge, gray sky.
I notice the snowflakes
Are all the same.
They don't look at all
Like the paper ones
We used to cut out
With dull, little scissors.
They look exactly alike.

Lonely?
Yes,
For the hayfields
That used to wrestle with me.
And my woolly children
That fell asleep
Under a voice of innocence.
Lonely,
For a dusty floor
And a plastic cup
Full of invisible tea.

Penelope Reedy

I AM A 4TH OR 5TH GENERATION Westerner, depending on which side of my family tree I draw upon. I'm about as western as a white woman can get. I've made playhouses out of the stumps of northwestern virgin timber; I've moved cattle on horseback and assisted at branding and dehorning "parties"; I've camped out alone and with friends and family; I can shoot pistols, rifles, and shotguns, and have hunted with each; I've shown Shoshone friends who have forgotten the old ways how to find and harvest Yampa root. Yet there has always been something inside of me which resists the power of the Western Myth to fix me within a rigid stereotype. And ironically, there has always been someone close to me—husband, cousin, sister-in-law, step-father—some more "typical" member of the western community, someone intent on copying and implementing the Myth to the hilt, who has insisted that because my interests vary widely in terms of literature, music, art, and friendships, I'm not a "real Westerner."

If I Left
by Penelope Reedy

he'd sit at the bar
and pout, while
divorcees with big tits
and dyed hair
flock around him claiming,
"All he needs is a good woman."

And elderly neighbor ladies
would bring casseroles
and jello salads
and pat him on the back.

If I left,
the gals at the supermarket
over coffee and a smoke
would say they knew it
would come to this
" . . . her, with 'the big head and all.'"

And if I stay,
and one day
draw a bead on his sweet brain
with the .44,
the men at the Club would say,
"We knew she was crazy."

And if I stay
until he shoots me,
catches me in the act of poetry,
barricaded behind a wall of books,
the Women's Auxiliary would say,
"She drove him to it."

Taco Sauce: 1982

by Penelope Reedy

I fold my apron
and prepare to catch my flight,
100 sagebrush miles to Boise
by night.

A dozen jars cool by the door.
I reach for my pen to label them
pausing at the final jar
fear of flight touching me.

In the air,
one place equals another.
It doesn't matter where you change.

As I write,
I envision hard-eyed men at the cafe
circling, circling my husband,
chanting the ancient mantra:
"Ya let a woman out,
she gets *the big head.*
Ya let a woman out—"

I grab the jar
and write:
"Taco Sauce: 1982
    First Wife"

Jeane Rhodes

Jeane Rhodes and Gwen Petersen were partners on the poetry trail until Jeane's death from cancer in 1987. Here, Gwen remembers her friend.

JEANE WAS MY BEST FRIEND, writing mentor, and appreciator for over twenty-five years. Jeane's wry eye lent itself to whatever we did. Once, on a trip to Canada, we spent road time making up a whole book's worth of limericks. Since we lived three hundred miles apart, we burned up telephone wires with calls and pestered our poor postal employees with masses of manuscript pages. We often collaborated, drawing from misadventures we had separately or together. A stickler for rhyme, meter and poetic feet, Jeane pounded poetry forms into my brain. "You can't even say the word chokecherries except in dactylic," she insisted—and wrote this poem to prove it.

Berry Me Not
by Jeane Rhodes

Chokecherries, chokecherries, purple and round.
How pleasant to live where these gems can be found.

My soulmate will love whatever I make,
Poured on a biscuit, or drowning a cake.

So, leaving a houseful of things to be done,
I grabbed up my buckets and vowed to have fun.

Off to the riverbank hot in pursuit
Of chokecherry bushes heavy with fruit—

I wasn't alone in the choice that I made,
Our cows were there too seeking water and shade.

Of course they had fertilized well where they lay,
So insects were thick on that scorching hot day.

But, darn it, I wasn't about to be licked
So I picked and I swatted and swatted and picked.

Then, both of my buckets heavy with loot,
I stepped in the mud as deep as my boot;

I followed it down with a face-forward sprawl—
Both buckets of chokecherries joined in the fall.

They silently sank in the cowpies and mud;
I picked up a few, they were covered with crud.

So back to the bushes, the heat and the bugs,
I picked them again, refilling my lugs.

Rushing back home, I started to cook,
Got dinner on somehow, by hook or by crook.

Washed all my berries and strained them for use,
Emptied my sugar sack into the juice.

It boiled for hours before it was ready;
I sterilized jars, I was getting unsteady.

I put on some supper, I cleaned up the mess,
And collapsed in a chair too tired to undress.

This morning my husband beamed over his plate
Of sausage and pancakes, and said as he ate,

"The best thing about this syrup to me
Is that these nice berries are utterly free."

To show that I'm tolerant and kind and forgiving—
The man that I live with is still with the living.

Edith Rylander

NORMALLY I WRITE SIX OR EIGHT poems a year, usually one at a time, often after long fore-thought. All of the lambing poems were written in one day. I was fully as groggy as "Dumb Animals" describes. The last of our ewes had an untreatably severe prolapse and was slowly bleeding to death. I sat down at the typewriter (normally I do poems in longhand) and started writing as fast as I could type. I would write a poem, go out and see if I could do anything for the dying ewe —I never could—and come back in and write another poem. It was a strange day.

Reaching In
by Edith Rylander

What goes on
Inside those wooly bodies
Whose wildness we bred out
Thousands of years back?
What are they thinking,
Those dark slit pupils
In the yellow eyes?

Three times now instead of the waterbag
And then the nose with feet
We've had the nose alone
Or the whole head with one foot, or none;
The legs up in there
Where the poor beast down on the straw
Can't free them by herself.

It's then you reach in, then
You put your care and all you know
Into the hot meat and terrible labor
Of that alien body,

Looking for the small soft foot,
And the slim doubled-back leg bones,
While around you the female muscles
Push and push like a bodily prayer;
Oh let it be born, oh let me be delivered.

Twice now I've worked it out, the hand thinking for
itself,
Til there's a shifting, a slither,
And then the lamb, with a great rush of birth-slime,
And a first small mutter of bleat; hurrah!

My hand feels different somehow when I wash it;
I have greater respect for my hand now than I used to.

Dumb Animals
by Edith Rylander

Ewes that bear full-sized well-formed lambs
And leave them unlicked, to die in the birth sac;
Ewes that clean them up and nurse them a couple of times,
And then decide the hell with it, and slam them across the pen
Against the barn wall;

And weakling lambs;
You kneel in straw, trying to get the lamb
To find the tit, the tit slipping from the mouth
Over and over;
The ewe collapsing, or circling, or kicking,
While you grab her, leaning a shoulder into dirty wool.
And the lambs that won't open their mouth
Into which you try to force nourishment
At three in the morning, in the sheep-smelling barn, groggy
for sleep,

Till you're ready to dump the beast back into the straw and
holler,
"Die, damn you, you stupid animal!"
And stump back under the stars to bed.

The limp body with the peppercorn wool
Is still breathing;
The heart still thumps in the chest
Small and distant
Like movement under the rubble
In a bombed building—

Take a deep breath. Start over.

The Firstborn
by Edith Rylander

The ewe with the partial prolapse of uterus and rectum
Struggled along five days.
We thought she was going to die.
We came close to shooting her
To end her misery.

On the fifth morning I found her
with the head of a big lamb completely out,
A white-face, with freckles,
Not in the birth-sack anymore, the tongue hanging,
but the nostrils and eyelids still trembling.

Both legs in. I couldn't feel legs or feet at all;
Only just above, right in the birth canal,
The lower jaw of a second lamb.
Nothing I did shifted anything,
And the ewe was exhausted.

Lorraine knows more about sheep than I do;
She went in and worked with all her patience
And practice. One foot, then the other,
Then it was out.
Limp as a scarf, cold and slimy
As a fish, hanging in my arms,
But the nostrils still quivering and the heart beating,
We hung it up by the heels to drain the crud out,
And I rubbed it down like crazy
While Lorraine helped pull the second,
A smaller lamb, a blackfaced buck.

We took them into the house and rubbed them by the woodstove
And ten minutes later the little blackface
Was wobbling around my kitchen;
When we hauled the ewe out to die
She flopped to her feet and started munching hay.
A week later you couldn't tell
There'd been anything wrong with her.

But the first, the whitefaced ewe lamb with the freckles
Was too long half-born.

She went to the back forty,
To the foxes and hawks and crows,
To the roots of blue violets.

Watching the Stuff on the News
by Edith Rylander

Watching the stuff on the news
All those well-groomed faces
Always saying the same things,
Guns mortars gas rockets bombs bombs bombs
I don't think we'll make it.

Watching the stuff on the news
On and on, the kids crying,
The old women beating their breasts, the young guys
Swaggering around with guns, "We will be revenged!"
I don't think we deserve to.

The big ewe in the end pen
Who was such a pain in the ass,
Knocking her water bucket down,
Blasting through the partition three times,
Drops twin lambs at nine below,
Talks to them, cleans them. Little bodies
Pouring out steam as if all their energy
Was boiling away—why don't they freeze?
They don't freeze;
In an hour they are clean and nursing.

Over the snow, under the same old stars,
Skunk smell at a distance. The first pungency of spring.
Something will make it, if not us;

Something will make it.

Out to Grass

by Edith Rylander

"The young lambs bound
As to the tabor's sound,"
Stiff legged, as if on springs;
The ewes catch the scent of new grass
And run with a bustling motion,
Udders bouncing, a few capering
Like their lambs,

But mostly tearing into the grass
With a greedy ripping of teeth.

The barn is empty;
The rubbing rags and bottles
Are put away till next year.
We have finished up the last
Of the lamb milk replacer.

Out to pasture, to be seen twice a day
When they get water and oats,
Are wool and hides and lamb-chops.

We can sleep through the whole night now.
We can study to make our lives
Worthy of what they eat.

Marie W. Smith

NEVER IN A MILLION YEARS would I have thought that a little red-haired girl, born and raised on a timber mill in the West Australian bush, would ever live on an American Ranch. Then, in May of 1950, I met a handsome American cowboy/artist, ready to serve a mission for the Mormon Church. Two years and one month later I found myself in an Idaho ranch house, cooking three meals a day, American style, for several hired men, my new husband and his father.

Writing is a longing I have had since the age of twelve or thirteen, when The Western Mail back in Australia turned down my first manuscript. The editor wrote a personal letter praising my work, but telling me to "write about what you know." At that age, I felt that anything I knew was frightfully boring. But the older I became, time seemed to press upon me the necessity to "leave something behind." Hence the quilts, the afghans, the photographs, the family records. I want to add to the list and leave something of the real me, my writing.

Finding
by Marie W. Smith

Love, my love, you are not gone from me,
for I see you in the face of all the land,
around autumn mountains snow tipped, free,

in waving seas of grain and verdant strand.
I feel you in the warm lake winds that blow
across the driftwooded, pebbled sand

and touch my cheek. Ah, love, if only I could go
where wild things fly alone and free,
find you above the dado glow

that separates our lives, our love and be
one again. To touch your outstretched hand—
a dream? Your strength I'd borrow, but reality

scorns the gift of presence loaned, demands
I just see you in the face of all the land.

The Diagnoses
by Marie W. Smith

Mrs. Lange's voice drifts
out of the bedroom window
onto the end of the front verandah
where Mum's begonias are blooming.
"Just watch him, Myrt.
If he bleeds from the bowels—"
She pauses.
I peer into the daylight darkness
of the bedroom.
She's shaking her large, shingled head.
"Well—you must hurry
to get him to the Doctor in time."
My belly hardens into a ball
I can feel with my fingers.
Mrs. Lange knows everything.
She was a British Army nurse
in the War.

I don't tell Mum that I have heard
because she never talks much
about things—like money,
or reasons for things,
or the sickness Billie has.
He is only six.
I am ten and now I know.
I have the same sickness.
Only I am worse.
The bleeding has already begun.
I don't have pain like he has,
but I dread to wake in the morning.
It is really bad then.
I try to stop it
but nothing lasts.

Via Satellite
by Marie W. Smith

Half a world away I hear,
after a millennium of seconds,
the tone I know is sounding near

her bed and I can see the nightstand phone
in the room she used to share
with my father. Not the home

of my childhood where I could stare
windows down at rainbows of Twenty-eights*
in wattle trees or cool bare feet across the floor

she carefully polished, then tugged all three
of us across its waxen glow,
us screaming for her to repeat . . .

the ringing stops. I wait to know
her voice again, hear her soft hello.

Catalogs
by Marie W. Smith

The little house was well supplied
no matter what the name.
There was Monkey Ward and Spiegel
and Sears, odd ones came
each year to brighten seasons
and keep alive the hope
of higher prices for the beef
so there'd be more than wire, rope

and staples and vet supplies.
Maybe a new red plaid shirt,
and something for the kids and her.
But then it'd really hurt
when I'd find them books so neatly piled
on the board that made the seat.
And I'd realize they was outdated
and I never did complete

the order form, cos I was waiting
for the check that never came
or when it did it was never enough
and I would always blame
myself and rip it,
crumple it with disgust,
then riffle through the pages
and find the treasures we had lost.

* colorful birds found in the West Australian Bush

Yes, It Was My Grandmother
by Luci Tapahonso

Yes, it was my grandmother
who trained wild horses for pleasure and pay.
People knew of her, saying:
> She knows how to handle them.
> Horses obey that woman.

She worked,
skirts flying, hair tied securely in the wind and dust.
She rode those animals hard and was thrown,
time and time again.
She worked until they were meek
and wanting to please.
> She came home at dusk,
> tired and dusty,
> smelling of sweat and horses.

She couldn't cook,
my father said smiling,
your grandmother hated to cook.

> Oh Grandmother,
> who freed me from cooking.
> Grandmother, you must have made sure
> I met a man who would not share the kitchen.

> I am small like you and
> do not protect my careless hair
> from wind or rain—it tangles often,
> Grandma, and it is wild and untrained.

THERE IS SUCH A LOVE OF STO-ries among Navajo people that it seems each time a group of more than two gather, the dialogue eventually evolves into sharing stories and memories, laughing, and teasing. To be included in this is a distinct way of showing affection and appreciation for each other. A person who is able to "talk beautifully" is well thought of and considered wealthy. To know stories, remember stories, and to retell them well is to have been "raised right."

Once my oldest brother said about my nálí, my paternal grandmother, who died decades ago: "She was a walking storybook. She was full of wisdom." Like many other relatives, she had a profound understanding of the function of language. I view my poems as a gift from my mother and father, both of whom embody the essence of Navajo elders—patience, wisdom, humor and courage. My poems are a collaboration of sorts with my sisters and brothers, my daughters and my husband, my extended family, and my friends. This writing, then, is not "mine," but a collection of many voices that range from centuries ago and continue into the future.

Sheepherder Blues

by Luci Tapahonso
for Betty Holyan

"Went to NCC for a year,"
she said,
"was alright.
There was some drinking, fights.
I just kept low.
It was alright."

This friend
haven't seen for a year or two.
It was a good surprise.
Took her downtown
to catch the next bus
to Gallup.

"I went to Oklahoma City,"
she said,
"to vacation, visit friends,
have a good time.
But I got the sheepherder blues
in Oklahoma City."

"I kept worrying about my sheep
if they were okay
really missed them,
the long days in the sun.
So after 4 days
I had to leave Oklahoma City."

So she went back,
first bus to Gallup,
then a 2-hour drive
to her sheep.

Raisin Eyes

by Luci Tapahonso

I saw my friend Ella
with a tall cowboy at the store
the other day in Shiprock.

Later, I asked her
Who's that guy anyway?

Oh Luci, she said (I knew what was coming).
It's terrible. He lives with me.
And my money and my car.
But just for awhile.
He's in AIRCA and rodeos a lot.
And I still work.

This rodeo business is getting to me
you know and I'm going to leave him
because I think all this I'm doing now
will pay off better somewhere else
but I just stay with him and it's hard
because

he just smiles that way you know
and then I end up paying entry fees
and putting shiny Tony Lamas on lay-away
again.
It's not hard.

But he doesn't know when
I'll leave him and I'll drive across the flat desert
from Red Rock in blue morning light
straight to Shiprock so easily.

And anyway
my car is already used to humming
a mourning song with Gary Stewart
complaining again of aching and breaking
down-and-out love affairs.

Damn.
These Navajo cowboys with raisin eyes
and pointed boots are just bad news
but it's so hard to remember that
all the time.

She said with a little laugh.

In 1864

by Luci Tapahonso

In 1864, 8,354 Navajos were forced to walk from Dinetah* to Bosque Redondo in
southern New Mexico, a distance of three hundred miles. They were held for four years
until the U.S. government declared the assimilation attempt a failure. More than
2,500 died of smallpox and other illnesses, depression, severe weather conditions, and
starvation. The survivors returned to Dinetah in June of 1868.

While the younger daughter slept, she dreamt of mountains,
the wide blue sky above, and friends laughing.

We talked as the day wore on. The stories and highway beneath
became a steady hum. The center lines were a blurred guide.
As we neared the turn to Fort Sumner,* I remembered this story:

A few winters ago, he worked as an electrician on a crew
installing power lines on the western plains of New Mexico.
He stayed in his pickup camper, which was connected to a generator.
The crew parked their trucks together and built a fire in the center.
The nights were cold and there weren't any trees to break the wind.
It snowed off and on, a quiet, still blanket. The land was like
he had imagined from the old stories—flat and dotted with shrubs.
The arroyos and washes cut through the soft dirt.
They were unsuspectingly deep.
During the day, the work was hard and the men were exhausted.
In the evenings, some went into the nearby town to eat and drink
a few beers. He fixed a small meal for himself and tried to relax.
Then at night, he heard cries and moans carried by the wind
and blowing snow. He heard the voices wavering and rising
in the darkness. He would turn over and pray, humming songs
he remembered from his childhood. The songs returned to him
as easily as if he had heard them that very afternoon.
He sang for himself, his family, and the people whose spirits
lingered on the plains, in the arroyos, and in the old windswept plants.
No one else heard the thin wailing.
After the third night, he unhooked his camper, signed his time card,
and started the drive north to home. He told the guys,
"Sure, the money's good. But I miss my kids and it sure gets lonely
out here for a family man." He couldn't stay there any longer.
The place contained the pain and cries of his relatives,
the confused and battered spirits of his own existence.

---

* *Dinetah* means "Navajo country" or "homeland of The People."

* Fort Sumner was also called "Bosque Redondo" owing to its location.

After we stopped for a Coke and chips, the storytelling resumed:

My aunt always started the story saying, "You are here
because of what happened to your great-grandmother long ago."

They began rounding up the people in the fall.
Some were lured into surrendering by offers of food, clothes,
and livestock. So many of us were starving and suffering
that year because the bilagáana* kept attacking us.
Kit Carson and his army had burned all the fields,
and they killed our sheep right in front of us.
We couldn't believe it. I covered my face and cried.
All my life, we had sheep. They were like our family.
It was then I knew our lives were in great danger.

We were all so afraid of that man, Redshirt,* and his army.
Some people hid in the foothills of the Chuska Mountains
and in Canyon de Chelly. Our family talked it over,
and we decided to go to this place. What would our lives
be like without sheep, crops, and land? At least, we thought
we would be safe from gunfire and our family would not starve.

The journey began, and the soldiers were all around us.
All of us walked, some carried babies. Little children and the elderly
stayed in the middle of the group. We walked steadily each day,
stopping only when the soldiers wanted to eat or rest.
We talked among ourselves and cried quietly.
We didn't know how far it was or even where we were going.
All that was certain was that we were leaving Dinetah, our home.
As the days went by, we grew more tired, and soon,
the journey was difficult for all of us, even the military.
And it was they who thought all this up.

We had such a long distance to cover.
Some old people fell behind, and they wouldn't let us go back to help them.
It was the saddest thing to see—my heart hurts so to remember that.

---

* *Bilagáana* is the Navajo word for Anglos.
* Kit Carson's name was "Redshirt" in Navajo.

Two women were near the time of the births of their babies,
and they had a hard time keeping up with the rest.
Some army men pulled them behind a huge rock, and we screamed out loud
when we heard the gunshots. The women didn't make a sound,
but we cried out loud for them and their babies.
I felt then that I would not live through everything.

When we crossed the Rio Grande, many people drowned.
We didn't know how to swim—there was hardly any water deep enough
to swim in at home. Some babies, children, and some of the older men
and women were swept away by the river current.
We must not ever forget their screams and the last we saw of them—
hands, a leg, or strands of hair floating.

There were many who died on the way to Hwééldi.* All the way
we told each other, "We will be strong as long as we are together."
I think that was what kept us alive. We believed in ourselves
and the old stories that the holy people had given us.
"This is why," she would say to us. "This is why we are here.
Because our grandparents prayed and grieved for us."

The car hums steadily, and my daughter is crying softly.
Tears stream down her face. She cannot speak. Then I tell her that
it was at Bosque Redondo the people learned to use flour and now
fry bread is considered to be the "traditional" Navajo bread.
It was there that we acquired a deep appreciation for strong coffee.
The women began to make long, tiered calico skirts
and fine velvet shirts for the men. They decorated their dark velvet
blouses with silver dimes, nickels, and quarters.
They had no use for money then.
It is always something to see—silver flashing in the sun
against dark velvet and black, black hair.

---

* Hwééldi is the Navajo name for Fort Sumner.

Myrt Wallis

Fear
by Myrt Wallis

Scared
Is running as fast as you can
With a wild-eyed cow blowing
Snot in your hip-pocket and
A faraway fence.

Scared
Is feeling your foot slip clean
Through the stirrup and knowing
You are bucked off if he
Takes one more jump.

Scared
Is hearing a rattler's buzz
In the dark barn, between
You and the light switch
And then another
By the door.

But nothing can touch
The bone-dread of
Masked marrow-suckers
Hovering above your
Drug-numb body.

Or the terror
Of waiting
For the verdict.

I WAS BORN ON THE CROW RESERvation in Montana and spent my early childhood there. My Dad was cow foreman and wagon boss for the Antler Ranch, so I am one of the lucky ones who got a firsthand look at that wonderful way of life. The rest of my growing up took place here in the Powder River Breaks of northern Wyoming. I attended the University of Wyoming until I met and married Dick Wallis, my husband of thirty-six years. We have always ranched, although we have also done a lot of other things on the side, to get our four children raised and educated. We have scaled down to a little place now, and are building a homestead, very slowly. With more time than money we are using logs and rocks from our land and doing the work ourselves. We have some very nice corrals and about three-fourths of a barn, so far. Hope to finish the barn and get started on a house this summer.

Bittercreek Women
by Myrt Wallis

Bittercreek has always been
A place of women
Getting by
Alone

Ann
Race horse husband
Off racing and dancing
She held the ranch together
Did all the work until
Old and crippled—legs useless
She improvised her kitchen
Crawled on hands and knees
To stay independent
And get by
Alone

Nellie
Widowed early
Wouldn't move to town
Called all her cows by name
Rode her old black horse in
Overalls and sunbonnet
Til she couldn't open gates
Paid off her place
Alone

Jennie
Divorced a weak man
To try to teach their mindless child
Fed herself and him by milking
Cows and tending hens
By some miracle
She got by
Alone

Lucinda
Abandoned with babies
On a homestead-size place
Raised 'em up fine on garden
Goods and haunches of deer left
On her step by neighbors at night
A candle in her window for twenty years
Was replaced by a little bed lamp
With a lacy shade for thirty more
Thinking he might
Come home
Sometime

Now there's me
And Billee and Gina
Bittercreek grass widows
Living on too-small places
Husbands off sending money home
Gina's Dusty gone trucking
Billee's man trading cows
Mine always someplace
Doing something

We get by
With our livestock and chores
Billee has singing, sewing and leather
Gina does canning, antiques and children
I have my reading and writing and garden
We talk on the phone to each other
But nights are long with aching
And wanting to be whole
Instead of half
Alone

Thaw
by Myrt Wallis

The south slope
Bares it's breast
Offering warmth and rest
I lie down with the cows
And winter comes
Out of my back
Like grubs.

Sue Wallis

WHILE I WAS IN GRADE school, my folks were feeding a thousand heifers in northern Wyoming. They accomplished this with a good team of Belgian work horses and a hay sled, and it took two days to get everything fed, up the creek one day, and down the next—all day long, day after day, until winter was done.

Since then, lots has changed. The big outfit is gone—lost to too much credit, and not enough rain for too many years—but my folks are still there on Bittercreek, hanging onto a chunk. My own life has taken a string of hard left turns, and I find myself now with a little family of my own, working in town, aching for space. Somewhere along the way I developed an almost religious reverence for the ways of my raising—the way we rode our colts, and built our gear, and threw our ropes, and tried to live our lives. Maybe these are ideas spawned from much loss, a nostalgic exile's point of view, but I think not. I think they have far more to do with a desire to hold fast to what is good, and true, and timeless.

Coyote Bitch
by Sue Wallis

Tonight . . .

I feel like a Coyote Bitch
(in heat)
Do not annoy me, tempt me, or toy with me
I have been lonely too long.

An old bitch will wait with native intellect
Run just below the ridges
You won't see her 'til she catches
That first waft of
Rottenness

She'll linger ruthless
Over the carrion carcass
Of some uncaring
Wild Steer

Then drag the stinking skin
Back to her solitary den
To chew and slobber and maul the hide
Long after all hint of flesh is dried

Just for comfort
Mangling idle dreams of regal wolfish lovers
Strong and smart and beautiful

. . . Who never appear.

Timothy Draw
by Sue Wallis

We pause at the top of Timothy Draw
Look down the country for stray cows
He cocks his head
Stands in the stirrups
Hands on the horn
Relaxed and easy and graceful
He moves with a horse
Like few men can

In one brief, quick space
I love him more
Than I will ever love again

Like passion, but not of sex
Like Life without death
Like the nudge and the tug and the sleepy smile
Of a too-full child at your still-full breast
Something that explodes from your toes
But flows through your bones
Like warm honey

More powerful than violence

    I lift my reins
    Our horses sidestep

    . . . and we slip on down the draw

Lead Mare
by Sue Wallis

That woman there
She can be a lead mare
Has watched horses so long
And so well she can tell what goes on
In their minds

It's that high-thrown head
How she holds her shoulders
Watch . . . she'll kinda hunch then
Throw her weight in ways
Unseen by us, but understood
By the saddle bunch

Once she tried it in Kentucky
that lead mare bit
And it worked there, too
At one of those fancy outfits
White board fences
Blooded thoroughbreds
She slipped away from the crowd
Stood quiet, moved her body
And they all quit grazing
Tossed her head
And they all came to her
Just like they do

At the ranch

To The Gauchas Of Salta
by Sue Wallis

My sisters of Salta
I know nothing of you,
but still I can see you
sitting straight in your saddles
cradled in sheepskin
with black and red ponchos
sweeping behind you
beneath flat, jaunty hats.

They write that your country
brutal breast of the Andes
rises out of the Pampas
in north Argentina.
And they write that you fought
fierce for your freedom,
that you rode hot and wild
alongside of your gauchos
in the war against Spain.

If I could but see you
in your low, green *montañas*
on vast, lonesome *estancias*
around *caballos* and *vacas*
maybe feel . . . of your homemade *riatas*
I know that we
would find much to speak of—

Like the prices of cattle
and the vagaries of lovers,
and how is it you make
a *criollo pingo*
spin light like a top,
and turn on the length of a hide.

I would show you my King rope,
my pictures of children,
we would talk about cooking,
about handling livestock,
the best ways to gather
in brushy cow country,
the places we've seen—
and speak of the merits of breeds
of good horses and cows.

There are no gauchas,
they say,
except for in Salta
where horsewomen ride
with pride and with flare.

Ah . . . my sisters of Salta
we have much to speak of.

[*Criollos* are the native wild horses descended from early
Spanish expeditions; *pingo* is a good horse.]

Mama Lessons
by Sue Wallis

"I first helped pull a calf . . . with my mother," Mama said,
But where I really learned of how to calve a heifer
Was having babies of my own—it wasn't anything I read,
Nor anything a fellow ever told me, that's for sure."

Mama's way was calm and easy, always careful with a cow.
Talking to them softly while she figured out the trouble.
"Take it easy, don't be wolfy, I'm here to help you, easy now—
Don't you hook me, little sister, I will help you while you double."

And Mama showed me how to drape the calving chains so very neat
"Kind of like the way you finger yarn when you are knitting,"
So you don't have any trouble when you're fishing for those feet
One-handed looping ankles in a cow that can't help fretting.

When the chains were fastened to the cable from the stretcher,
"Just snug it up, don't really pull, just keep a little tension
On the chain," my Mama said, "we'll wait and then we'll help her
When it is the proper time—we will pull with her contraction."

"Most fellows that I've seen," she said, "have no consideration
For a cow and go to cranking, yank it out in spite of her.
They don't care, or perhaps, a man can't understand the situation—
Male logic always tells them that the quicker is the better."

"But . . . there's a surge and ebbing that can never be denied.
The labor comes and then you Work—make all the progress that you can—
The space between is rest, when energy revives
For another total effort, all out effort, as the labor comes again."

"So listen to that rhythm, Dear, it's how you help the best.
Often Life demands of us some Patience and an understanding Will.
Learn to follow Nature's way—know when to work and when to rest—
Take it easy, treat her gently, and when she pushes . . . crank like Hell."

Thus my Mama's mother taught her, and then my Mama taught to me
The important things of birthing and of Life and Nature's ways—
Of the knowledge wise and female—first so given to me free
By my mother in a pasture on those long-passed calving days.

I have tried to tie my living to Life rhythms that work best,
Tried to find that Patience, and to cultivate that Will,
I have tried to take it easy—learn when to work and when to rest—
Like my Mama treat them gently, and when it's time . . . to work like Hell.

I WISH TO THANK MADGE BAIRD, JOHN DOFFLEMYER, Paul Zarzyski, and Hal Cannon, whose wisdom and generosity made this project possible, and the staff of the Western Folklife Center, who graciously responded to dozens of queries. My deepest gratitude is to the many poets featured here who gave of their good work and also their time to make this book a reality.

—Teresa Jordan, Editor

GRETEL EHRLICH: "For David," "The Orchard," and "Born in the Afternoon" from *To Touch the Water*, ©1981 by Gretel Ehrlich, published by Ahsahta Press. All poems used with permission of the author. Introductory remarks from *"The Solace of Open Spaces,"* from The Solace of Open Spaces, © 1985 by Gretel Ehrlich. Used with permission of Viking Penguin, a division of Penguin Books USA Inc.

MARTHA DOWNER ELLIS: "Happy Birthday" and "Never Let Us Think" reprinted from *Bell Ranch Glimpses*, © 1980 by Martha Downer Ellis. Used with permission of the author, Ellis Books, c/o George F. Ellis, Rt. 1, Box 220, Eagle Pass, TX.

JUNE BRANDER GILMAN AND HELEN KAY BRANDER: "People Will Talk" from *Rhymes of Today and Yesterday*, © 1987 by June Brander Gilman. Used with permission of June Brander Gilman.

PEGGY GODFREY: "Old Vogal" was first published in *Dry Crik Review*, Winter 1992, © 1992 by Peggy Godfrey; "Roland" and "Perfect Wife" from *Write 'Em Cowgirl*, © 1993 by Peggy Godfrey. All poems used with permission of the author.

AUDREY HANKINS: "Relapse" first published in *Dry Crik Review*, Winter 1992, © 1992 by Audrey Hankins. Used with permission of the author.

LINDA HASSELSTROM: "Beef Eater" and introductory comments reprinted from *Land Circle: Writings Collected from the Land*, © by Linda Hasselstrom, Fulcrum Publishing, Inc., 350 Indiana St., #350, Golden, CO 80401. Used with permission of the publisher. "Planting Peas," "Rancher Roulette," "Seasons in South Dakota" and "Driving Into a Storm" reprinted from *Dakota Bones: The Collected Poems of Linda Hasselstrom*, © 1993 by Linda Hasselstrom, published by Spoon River Poetry Press. Used with permission of the author.

JOAN HOFFMAN: "New Ranch Wife," "The Lonely, Empty, Prairie Sky," "Helen," "I Remember Being Beautiful," and "Remembering Willie Mae," © 1994 by Joan Hoffman. Used with permission of the author.

LINDA HOGAN: Introductory comments, "Celebration: Birth of a Colt," and "Left Hand Canyon" reprinted from *Red Clay*, © 1991 by Linda Hogan, published by The Greenfield Review Press. "The Other Voices" reprinted from *Savings*, © 1988 by Linda Hogan, published by Coffee House Press. All selections used with permission of the author.

LINDA HUSSA: "The Blue Filly" was first published in *Dry Crik Review*, Spring 1993, © 1993 by Linda Hussa. "Homestead in Hell Creek Canyon," "Under the Hunter Moon," "Homesteaders, Poor and Dry," and "The Widow Olson" © 1994 by Linda Hussa. All poems used with permission of the author.

MARGOT LIBERTY: "Evening, Four Mile," "Rain Prayer," and "Epitaph" © 1994 by Margot Liberty. Used with permission of the author.

JO-ANN MAPSON: "Spooking the Horses" and "Tell Us Again" from *Spooking the Horses*, © 1991 by Jo-Ann Mapson, published by Thunder and Thistle Press. "Graining the Mare" was first published in *Dry Crik Review*, Winter 1992, © 1992 by Jo-Ann Mapson. All poems used with permission of the author.

MELA D. MLEKUSH: "The Rummage Sale" and "Gentleman of the Prairie" © 1994 by Mela D. Mlekush. Used with permission of the author.

JENNIFER OLDS: "A Wild One Goes" and "Blinding the Infidel" from *The Half Acre Ranch*, © 1992 by Jennifer Olds, published by First Editions Press. Used with permission of the author.

VERLENA ORR: "First Job" first appeared in *Slow Dancer*, February 1991, © 1991 by Verlena Orr. "Our Mother's Mother" first appeared in *Snap Dragon*, August 1985, © 1985 by Verlena Orr. "Prophe-

Photographs by Teresa Jordan